I0822734

Blue River

ZINAIDA LONGORTOVA

The best work in the literary competition
"Open Eurasia Book Forum and Literature Festival - 2015"

Published in United Kingdom
Hertfordshire Press Ltd © 2016

9 Cherry Bank, Chapel Street
Hemel Hempstead, Herts.
HP2 5DE, United Kingdom
e-mail: *publisher@hertfordshirepress.com*
www.hertfordshirepress.com

Blue River

by Zinaida Longortova©

English - Khanty

Translated by Anna Kotova & Charles Van Der Leeuw
Edited by Stephen M. Bland
Design by Aleksandra Vlasova
Typeset of Khanty version by Palina Vilava
Project manager Anna Lari

British Library Catalogue in Publication Data
A catalogue record for this book is available from the British Library Library of Congress in Publication Data
A catalogue record for this book has been requested

ISBN 978-1-910886-34-2

Contents

Prologue

Each person's will to live and to create is what gives me inspiration. And in spite of having grown up a long time ago, I still remember every moment of my childhood. In this tale, I wish to share my cherished recollections about the short but happy time I spent with a young elk.

In Kushevat, one can see the splendor of myriad species of wildflowers in full bloom during different parts of the summer. As soon as the earth reveals itself, removing its blanket of snow in the spring, tender green grass appears. The yellow-faced mother and stepmother wake before the last spot of snow has melted. Summer is on its way at last, and shortly it will be time for the *vonzi*[1]. The middle of June is spawning time on the wetlands for the beautiful nelma fish, along with all the other breeds.

Fish and birds, as well as humans, have a tendency to return to the places where they were born. For me, Kushevat

---

1 *The yearly swimming of fish upstream*

is the most wonderful place on Earth. Whenever I see a place with similarities, my heart fills and I indulge in my sweet memories.

Once I happened to visit Karelia, and there on the sacred island of Kizhi, it was just like my homeland. The sun was shining and the fields were covered in buttercups, cornflowers and soft, woolly grass. Bells were ringing, suggesting some regional ritual was taking place. It felt to me as though I was walking the paths of my tiny motherland. That piece of earth on which I was born gives me strength. Small, almost forgotten, but boasting a rich history, the village of Kushevat was for a long time probably only native soil to the Khanty, but in my memory, the place was home to many different peoples. Beyond the trickling Saimas River, there was a mansion, and atop the high hill above it stood what used to be the Holy Trinity Church, the type of which hundreds can be found. My family lived in Kushevat. The church was right behind our house, lingering in a state of disrepair with holes where the windows had once been. We Khanty children were not allowed in there. For the adults, even an abandoned church remained a sacred place. I cannot recall what its walls looked like, but during my mother's childhood the Khanty used to call it the Red Sacred House. It stood out against a backdrop of clear blue sky.

I was born in Kushevat in June 1962, in the days of the Soviets. My childhood drifted past in a calm and peaceful manner. All around grew ancient evergreen cedars.

The smell of pine needles is the scent of my youth, but the trees also blossomed, scarlet and sweet.

When I was little, children were not allowed to enter neighbouring yards. It was considered a sign of a bad upbringing, an indecency to wander into somebody else's house for no reason. For seven years, my brother and I had little contact with other children; and although we wished very much to play with them, the thought of disobeying the rules set by the adults never crossed our minds. Occasionally we spotted children of our age by peering over fences, but we only interacted with them when our grandmother took us on a visit. When neighbours with children came to our home, it was like a feast. We gave them our finest dolls, showed them the largest cedar nuts and treated them to fresh milk. Our joy seemed endless.

The house and the space in the birch wood *chums*[2] which grandmother put up in the summer were our domain. This is where my childhood days rolled by, with the sweet smell of blooming herbs in summer and the white snow and frosts of minus forty degrees in winter. I remember those years as both solar and serene, with eight months of ice hiding the sky as though it wanted it to vanquish it from one's memory, and the two short months of glorious sun which we would cling onto for dear life.

Whenever I recall my childhood in Kushevat, the mental storms ravaging through my mind ease, and I feel an urge to press myself upon the cool ground and watch the

2 *Summer tent*

butterflies flying from flower to flower. To reach out a hand to a ladybug in order for it to rest upon it, and feel content that there is a piece of earth that gives one strength and confidence in the future. Whenever times are hard or I need a space to contemplate, if possible I return to the home where my little long-legged friend would brush against me asking me for a slice of bread. These are the memories that I want to share with you.

My long-legged Friend

Pitlor ran, her heart beating fast. The young elk had been overfeeding on biscuits and candies, she cried out, and now he was dying.

On Sundays, people from neighbouring settlements used to come to visit, always bringing something tasty with them. They knew about the elk and were eager to see the wild, tender and kind animal. It gratefully accepted their gifts. That Sunday, guests had come to the village in larger numbers than usual, leaving an abundance of confections.

The girl had stopped abruptly at the corner of the house as she saw her Uncle Yukhur, with the elk lying on the ground next to him. Her kindly uncle stroked the animal's swollen stomach. The horror of the sight stiffened her legs as though they were wooden stilts. Gingerly, she approached and tapped her *aka*[3] on the shoulder, asking him what had happened. Her uncle briefly raised his grief-stricken eyes

---

3 *Uncle*

filled with unshed tears, then lowered them as though not to wanting to show too much of his feelings to the young girl. His resolve breaking, his tears fell on the *kuran*[4] lying in front of him. Shaking helplessly, he raised his eyelids, but the world no more than a blur to him, he quickly closed them again. Next to him, the long legs of the elk lay motionless.

The girl's breast heaved so violently that she found it hard to breathe. She had wanted to go to the club to watch a movie called *Fire, Water and Copper pipes*, but instead she had run across her uncle, her heart sinking as she looked at his face. Used to seeing him mirthful and the elk strong and kicking, she squeezed her hands into fists. She understood without her uncle saying the pain he was in. Tense and pale, Yukhur kept rubbing the elk's muscles. He would rather die, he thought, than part with the animal. Overwhelmed by grief, he remained speechless and could not face his niece. Massaging the elk's stomach, he moved his hands mechanically, but the animal didn't stir.

An overwhelming sense of despair gripped the girl and she ran off over the hill and down into the valley. She sprinted through the settlement, which now seemed endlessly vast, until she came to the edge of the woods. Darting through the trees, she following a narrow footpath, unmindful of the terrible things that could happen in that gloomy place. Silent tears poured from her eyes as they had from Uncle Yukhur's, falling onto her scarf. Usually, Pitlor spoke loudly to get the attention of adults, but here she was

4 *Literally, an animal with long legs*

alone with her tears. From time to time, she looked around to see if anyone was watching her, and then ran further into the forest. Sadness overcame her little heart. Never before had she felt such pain and fear.

She raced through a stream, not noticing the hummocks distinguished by the different type of grass over which one should jump lest one stumble and fall into the water. Tumbling with a loud and desperate cry, Pitlor lay there barely noticing the chill water surrounding her. Winding between the hummocks, the forest stream flowed on into the wild and deep River Ob, which carried away the little girl's tears. Withdrawing to a dry place, finally Pitlor calmed down a little, squeezed out her wet clothes and started to wander towards home.

***

Two and a half years before, at the start of June, the young man Yukhur, in his early twenties, came back from fishing. He had put up a series of nets to catch the local *litsa* fish[5]. In his ears, above the sound of the roaring waters of the Ob, he could still hear his old mother say "Do not forget, my son, to wet your hair and to wash your face in the sacred waters."

The previous day, the river had cast off its winter shield of ice. It was time to honour the great water goddess Yik Ur, while floating on the river which represented her sacred

5 *A freshwater fish of the carp family*

body. And even though Yukhur knew the ancient tradition of worshipping the hallowed waters, it touched him to be reminded of it by his mother, who showed her love for him in this manner. After having wet his hair wet and washed his face, therefore, he muttered the spell: Ushch – howl, pot, pot, pot[6] and jumped into the boat.

A mild breeze stirred his cloth hood and ruffled his curly black hair. The open, hearty image of northerners was reflected in Yukhur's character, but he also had something special about him which distinguished him from his fellow villagers. The young man's attractive round face, darkened by the sun, radiated his kindness and trustworthiness. His honesty had gained Yukhur, though still a young man, respect among his companions and the administrators from the state fisheries agency. He was one to be relied upon, which was why that spring morning on a public holiday, the director of the state farming unit, Gregory Yakovlevich Sayenko had awarded him the Certificate of Honour and tasked him with executing the annual plan for the collection of furs. The grant which accompanied the award was used by Yukhur to buy a new engine for his boat, which he had named "Breeze". Such a strong engine was to be found nowhere else in the village, and only people of special merit were allowed to buy and maintain one.

The Ob had started breathing again, ridding itself of the burden of its winter clothes. Enjoying the spring day, Yukhur skillfully steered the motorboat, circumventing the

6 *In the Khanty proverb, the Ob River and its tributaries are compared to oil or grease on which fish rise to spawn*

last remaining ice floes. Then, in a sudden frenzy, a storm broke, smashing everything in its path and breaking the ice with burning tentacles. It was thus that the all-devouring monster, Yalan Iki[7] destroyed anything it found in its course. The raging ice floes hitting the shore careened into trees and bushes, ripping them up by the roots. Starved by the winter, Yalan Iki was now roaring with no sign of becoming sated. Nothing could escape from this mighty creature, his raging hunger and masses of broken ice.

Approaching the banks of the Ob, Yukhur spotted a she-elk in some distress. When he finally made it ashore, he saw an elk calf stuck in the branches of a felled tree. The elk's mother fled in terror upon seeing the boat, leaving the calf to this well-meaning benefactor.

Mooring his boat on an uprooted tree, Yukhur disentangled the young animal.

"Run, run after your mother!" he cried. "Why do you not hurry?"

But it appeared that the calf had hurt its foot and could not even stand.In the Khanty proverb, the Ob River and its tributaries are compared to oil or grease on which fish rise to spawn.

Lifting the shivering calf from the water, Yukhur placed it in his boat and covered it with a raincoat. Well, he thought, it didn't drown is the main thing. At least it's alive, and its foot I can heal. We shall soon be friends. He will miss his mother, of course, which is awful, but she's a long way

7 *Mythical evil spirit that resides in the forest*

off now and unable to help him. So starting the engine of Breeze, he glided back towards the village.

Playing games under the beaming sun, Yukhur's niece and nephew noticed the strange couple as their uncle approached, carefully carrying something with long, thin dangling legs. The wounded animal shivered all over upon seeing the strangers, the children staring in amazement at the calf and wondering what it was. A foal, perhaps? But then why the long legs? And how to explain the small hump on its back? And what an attractive face! No, this was no foal. As they crowded round, Yukhur remained silent, a mysterious radiance shining from his face. This glow emanating from their uncle intrigued the children so much that it rendered them speechless.

After carefully laying the calf on a bale of hay in his house, Yukhur turned to address his niece and nephew.

"Run to your grandmother," he ordered them. "Ask her for a bottle of boiled milk with a teat."

"*Unanki*!"[8] the children cried to their grandmother. "Aka brought home a wounded animal and is asking for boiled milk in a bottle with a teat, such as we use for calves."

Grandmother, who was hard to surprise, had no boiled milk at hand, but instead gave them a bottle of delicious sweetened tea with milk. She then took a kettle, poured some fresh milk into it and placed it on the stove to boil. Having noticed the events from a distance, she understood that the calf needed help. She knew that her young son,

8 *Grandmother*

Yukhur, her comfort and hope in her old age, would never leave either a person or an animal in distress, and deep inside she felt very proud of him.

Having darted back, Pitlor and her brother Sorjyokhan saw the animal with its leg already in a splint, their uncle having attached a bandage to a small piece of board. Taking the bottle from the children, he dripped the tea from the teat onto young elks' lips. At first, the calf shook its head so fiercely that the drops scattered in all directions. He even got some of the liquid in his nose, while gazing mournfully at the children as if to say: Just look at me, my sorry state, upon which he sneezed loudly. Happy as a child himself because of the lovely creature he'd found, Yukhur once more poured some drops on its lips, this time more successfully. Sticking out his tongue to absorb the liquid from his nose, the calf, it seemed, now wished to drink. Soon his lips had clutched the teat.

Though they were only six years old, the children already had some experience in feeding animals. Last spring, they had brought up a bull-calf after the cow Dawn had calved, and then a female calf, Zorki, after her mother Marta had calved. The children skillfully handled the milk bottle, even though the little animals, somehow always hungry, sometimes knocked them down. Horses especially would show themselves reluctant to admit them to their young and confined them to mare's milk. This spring, their house was full of animals – even Shchap the dog had little ones.

In these parts, it was possible to play with the deer – such lands still exist.

And so there was the calf with Uncle Yukhur, taciturn and mysterious, his silence somehow speaking of wisdom. At last, after having fed the shivering little elk, Yukhur explained to the children:

"This is a wild animal from the forest; in the Khanty language it is called a kuran. It got tangled in the branches of a felled tree and broke its leg, which is why his mother has entrusted him to us. He will not recover unless you look after him with care; you agree?"

Their eyes shining with delight, the children cried out to grandmother, interrupting one another as she entered the house.

"Unanki, give me a small bottle of milk!"

"There's no need to fight over it," grandmother responded, "or else I shall feed it myself. Let Sorjyokhan feed him first; after all, he is a boy. As for you, my dear Pitlor, you shall feed Uncle Yukhur in the evening. I will help you, all right?"

Although disappointed, the girl agreed, it being the custom that the boy in the family should carry out such a task first for the simple reason that he was a boy. So running off, Sorjyokhan brought back a deer skin which grandmother had taken from her entrance hall, and together with his uncle he placed it under the elk so he would not be tormented by the cold soil.

As spring embraced everything with warm rays of sunlight, the young elk soon found comfort in the kind caresses of the children's tender hands. The boy and the girl were gifted a small playground on the banks of the stately River Ob, which carried its waters to the Kara Sea. Everything at this time of year breeds happiness, and the earth, woken in excitement, indulges in the tender beams of *Nye-Imi*,[9] reaching out and absorbing the rays in her breast, which had become stiff after the long winter. From under the already waning permafrost, plumes of fresh grass were already waiting to spurt. Summer was steadily moving towards her hour of glory.

In a week's time, the young elk was already cantering, the siblings holding the bottle of milk for the animal to drink from after it had caught up with them. At first, the calf moved with a limp, but thanks to his long legs, he soon managed to make a run for it so that he could receive his treat. The children gathered the first shoots of grass for him, but he turned away from it, preferring his bottle of milk.

"Longlegs, that is what we shall call you!" the children shouted, trying to push a bunch of grass into his mouth. "But if you don't eat this, you won't grow up!"

Though the children played with the animal, most of the latter's heart went out to his savior. Uncle Yukhur treated the calf as if it were his own child. If his niece and nephew could at times forget to feed the young elk, he never would. He kneaded it on its withers and brushed its hair. The young

9 *The Khanty name for the Sun Goddess*

man pitied the young animal. He had no mother to look after him, so all his love went out to Uncle Yukhur. When his master returned from fishing, Longlegs soon forgot his little friends and rushed towards the riverbank at full speed. And whenever Yukhur was away, Pitlor's mother was there to feed him. She looked after all the animals and never left Longlegs unattended.

During the hottest month of the summer, grandmother put up birch wood chums in the yard. Inside them, the nights were cooler and one wasn't so haunted by the mosquitoes' aggression. Uncle Yukhur also made his dwelling in a birch wood shelter. Every evening when he went to bed, as though ignoring the young elk he pulled down the curtains made of goose wings in order to keep the mosquitoes out. From their bedroom window, the children looked curiously into the yard to see what happened, and every night their uncle quietly raised the curtains, the young elk rising on all fours and slipping inside. There he slept peacefully all night long. Knowing her son's whims, grandmother mumbled that it was impossible to raise and keep a wild animal, but sympathy made her quietly go to bed and the practice continued.

Naturally, the children wanted to sleep together with their uncle and the young elk, but they were strictly forbidden to do so. Here, grandmother was determined.

"Aka needs to have his rest," she would tell them, "for tomorrow he has a lot of work to do. At five in the morning, there are twenty nets that must be checked, and you will prevent the state plan from being carried out!"

For a long time, the children would peep into the yard while the blazing sun was waiting to set. They would fall asleep whilst Nye-Imi was resting on the horizon, her light shining on the silver-blue waters of the Ob. Taking a brief respite from her day's labour, but never disappearing, clad in gold the sun would begin her journey across the eternal sky once more. In summer, she has no time to rest, for she would hibernate through the entire winter.

In the afternoon, Pitlor and Sorjyokhan would go to the treeless islet of Harypata, where the cows are kept away from mosquitoes. Not wishing to stay home, Longlegs would sprint after them, like a little dog begging for milk and bread. The children were as nimble as foxes, but the kuran always caught up with them when it was time to drive the cows home for milking. As Pitlor's mother sat down to milk a cow next to the house, the young elk waited for the first streams of milk to appear, then started to nudge her as though he wanted to say: "don't forget me; I'm here and I'm hungry!" The happy elk soon devoured his pail of milk, after which he ran back to grandmother's house.

Unanki always carried some slices of bread with her, hidden in the front pocket of her wide and colourful dress.

"Eat your bread, but not too much. It is your treat," she said, gently caressing the animal. "You are little and sweet, as are your friends, but their favourite food is chocolate and they will never refuse it. You don't need that fatty stuff, you're fine having bread."

The young elk laboriously chewed on a slice of bread, half of which fell out of his mouth. Carefully picking the remaining piece up, he finished his meal, lay down beside the stove on which grandmother was busy preparing food for the winter and dozed off. His hostess's home was always quiet and comfortable, and there was always something to feed upon. A veil of smoke from the stove soon shrouded the clearing, protecting it from mosquitoes and midges.

"Do not offend Longlegs," grandmother asked the children while frying a *shumakha* fish until it was golden brown. "Your friend has protectors who watch over him lest you are not good to him."

"And who are his protectors?" the children eagerly asked.

"The Great Turam[10] itself and his *Lunkhat*[11] watch over the young elks. Our people have sacred animals, certain birds and insects which mustn't be attacked. Thus, it is not allowed to offend a frog sitting on a mound, a dragonfly or an eagle, as well as many other kinds of animals. Remember what harm befell us after you threw stones at a frog?"

"Grandmother, we shall not do that again, we did not know," the children protested. "We were afraid that our little elk would eat the frog alive."

The children remembered well the day when Longlegs had found a frog in the grass, which had drawn his attention by its jumping. Without knowing what kind of creature it was, Longlegs ran after it to catch it. The children thought

---

10 *The Sun, the supreme god in the mythology of the Khanty*
11 *Divine guardian spirit*

that the calf wanted to eat the frog and were alarmed by the idea that their friend would have a frog jumping up and down in his stomach. To prevent that, they threw sticks and stones in the frog's direction. Perhaps they had killed it, or maybe it had escaped, they did not know, but they had offended the frog.

That very same evening, Pitlor's mother was taken ill. She panted, as though something in her breast was disturbing her. Deeply alarmed for the sake of her daughter, grandmother had asked the children whether they had seen any frogs. Only the offspring of the goddess of the great waters, Yik Urr can penetrate into a person's chest and make it impossible for them to breathe, but who had provoked the goddess' wrath towards her daughter? Fearing for her mother's life, Pitlor admitted everything.

That night nobody slept. Grandmother ordered her son to cast a frog made of metal, and till morning she prayed to the Great Turam and Yik Urr to forgive the children's folly. Cutting a hollow in the shape of a frog into a piece of birch wood, Uncle Yukhur poured melted copper into it. The children watched how the copper took the form of a frog. Once it had cooled, Uncle Yukhur gave the model to the guilt-ridden children's grandmother, who wrapped it in a beautiful coloured scarf. Yukhur then climbed onto the rooftop and placed the metal frog, sitting on the scarf, onto the roof in order to reconcile the spirits.

The events having petrified the children, Pitlor buzzed around her mother like a moth asking Yik Urr for pardon.

Grandmother held a ceremony in the sacred corner of the house for Yik Orr's offspring. Only then she would let the other members of the household go to bed, but she remained up to attend to her daughter. When the children rose the next morning, they saw their mother looking pale, but in good health and already back from her milking round. From now on, whenever they saw a frog, they would stay far away from it.

"When I was a child, just a little older than you are now," grandmother told them, "hunters brought the carcass of a younger brother[12] home, after which worshipping ceremonies were held. For seven days, holy songs were sung in the honour of the divine beast. I recall how a similar ritual took place when hunters brought an elk's meat home. We Khanty are not pescatarians who can live without meat and feed on fish alone, but we have to honour the animal to comfort the rotating sun in her sorrow. If you look at the sky in fall as it gets darker, you will see the image of Longlegs in the stars."

Warming to her tales, grandmother turned to the next ancient legend.

"One day, three men were in pursuit of a long-legged elk. The animal was very tired, but it did not wish to perish, so with its last bit of strength, he ran deep into the snow attempting to separate himself from the swift-footed hunters. The Great Turam appeared in the form of a white snow deer and watched the elk's struggle to escape. At last,

---

12 *The Khanty term for a bear*

he felt so sorry for the animal that he lifted it up and placed it in the sky. The huntsmen remained without game."

"Unanki, why is it that so many animals, birds and insects are sacred and cannot be harmed?"

"Because together they form a large family of divine protectors who keep us safe from trouble," she answered, "and if you offend one of them, their protector can make life very hard."

Whilst she spoke the old woman never stopped skinning fish after fish, which she hung on a line in a long row to dry. She kept cooking with her skillful, wizened hands, ignoring the mosquitoes, midges and the scorching sun, for fish is quick to spoil.

"All life here is preserved by Nye, who appears in the image of a black cat," she continued. "The supreme goddess is Qassam-Nye, and granddaughters are protected by Lev Kutap Iki, one of the sons of Great Turam."

"Does that mean that somehow the offspring of an elk cow protects people's destiny as well?" Pitlor asked.

"That's correct," grandmother replied. "Maybe they live far away from our village, but once an animal is considered sacred, so is its offspring, its entire breed. And you also have a protector, a *vruchenka*."[13]

"I know, I know," Pitlor squealed in delight, "that's the offspring of a coloured dog, as you told me before. Therefore, I never harm any dogs."

"Yes, Elyan Aura and Hanshan Aura protect you and

13 *Sacred coloured dog*

at times, so we never harm them and we feed the puppies."

"I shall be sure to feed them at all times!"

"Now pay attention," grandmother said, cleaning the fish board. "This whole week the Old Men have been standing on the horizon, lightly lashing their whips. You hear some rustling, some rattling, and then silence. The rains are closing in on us. My legs ache and ache."

"Grandmother, which old men are you speaking about?" Sorjyokhan asked. "There are no old men in the village."

"I am talking about the Old Men of the Sky, my grandchildren. Closely behind the clouds they appear, and for a week now the cool clouds have been gathering. Ah, those Old Men!"

The children peered at the blue-black horizon and drew back. Pitlor and Sorjyokhan were afraid of these Old Men, rumbling as though the Ural Mountains were collapsing.

"Cover your heads with cloth, you cannot go out in a rainstorm without wearing a headscarf, or your hair will turn gray before its time," grandmother warned them. "Since ancient days, the bald Old Men of the Sky have demanded respect, and you cannot approach them bare-headed. Your legs are still young. Now run for it, and look for a *bez-nozha-legayushchego-dyaduyshi*, a dragonfly heralding rain. The dragonfly is on friendly terms with the Old Men. In a day, rain will fall and my legs will feel less painful. Remember last year I told you this verse:

Dragonfly, dragonfly,
Five hundred times you drank my blood!
Six hundred times you drank my blood!
Now, therefore, ask the Old Men
For rain clouds!

"Why are your sore legs, unanki?" Pitlor asked, placing her small handles on her grandmother's knees, hoping to ease the pain.

"I fell the other day, hurting my knees a little, but now they're not so bad really. Your legs are young, so you can run, but with legs you never know what you're in for. Now go, bring a piece of fish to the old lady next door as a gift."

The children, who had just finished their lunch sprang to their feet at this command. Every day when they visited Vatushka's house carrying fish, they were treated to tea and sweets, and here they were having eaten so lavishly they could not stomach any more. Why did grandmother always send them bearing milk or fish to the neighbour's house right after lunch? Better do it before lunch! But there was nothing they could do, so the children ran towards Vatushka's.

"Wait! I forgot to give you curdled milk to take to the old woman. She likes it very much!" grandmother cried.

But the children did not hear her anymore; they would need to return later.

"What's the hurry?" unanki sighed.

The children darted along the footpath, on either side

of which dragonflies flew up, the messengers of rain. Having almost hurtled into one, Pitlor threw herself to one side and landed in the dense grass. The fish flew into the air, but showing no intention of leaving, the dragonfly landed close by.

"*Shchyokhra, hukhra oakhan ik!* Dragonfly, dragonfly, I implore you, bring rain from the Old Men of the Sky!" the girl whispered, afraid to scare off the insect. "My grandmother's knees hurt very much, and if the rain arrives her pain will go. Fly to the Old Men and inform them, so they will make it rain."

As though taking heed of her request, the dragonfly took flight from the leaf on which it had been sitting and set off for realms unknown. Picking up the piece of fish, Pitlor ran to catch up with her brother, wondering whether the dragonfly had understood her message.

Welcoming her guests, the old lady Vatushka set up a small table in the middle of the room for a modest lunch to be followed by candies and gingerbread. Vatushka lived alone and was always glad to talk to the children, but she knew that the fish should be prepared, so after asking for news from the community, she let her guests return home.

In the late afternoon, the sky darkened and a terrible rumbling could be heard. Firmly closing the fences, grandmother herded the children indoors.

"The Old Men of the Sky have lashed their horses on the backside, within the hour the horses will trot," she said. "It's clear that the dragonfly you spoke to has passed the message onto the Old Men and now the rain is gathering."

She'd hardly managed to close the door behind them before the rain started to pound upon the house.

Autumn Adventures

It was a clear, sunny day. As people would stop to visit unanki on their way to the little country shop, crossing the small stream that divided the village, word had come that the Jalaps, the teachers from the boarding school had come to announce that all the older children would have to go to boarding school the following week. At the same time, a large barge had arrived carrying a variety of winter provisions for the village. Together, Pitlor, her mother, Sorjyokhan and their grandmother went to the shop, the children cheerfully hoping for gifts. Also there, the young elk was mingling with the crowd.

"Our Longlegs is here wishing to receive a surprise," people joked.

"Anka!,"[14] Pitlor cried, rushing up to her mother who was waiting in the queue. "Let us buy cloth and I shall sow a collar with beads for our poor little elk. Buy red beads."

---

14 *Mother*

"We shall, we shall," her mother said, pacifying her. "Not just red but green as well, and then your grandmother will teach you how to do the artwork.

"I shall buy the beads for you," unanki said to the girl, gently taking her granddaughter's palm in her rough, calloused hand. "You will sew some beautiful patterns for your friend."

Gripping her grandmother's hand, Pitlor calmed down a little, even though amidst the excited throng it was hard to do so.

Grandmother took a number of marked boxes that had come from the warehouse, the contents of which she was allowed to distribute as they contained gifts for relatives. Watching how her grandmother had circumvented the system, the girl ran to the young elk and grasping him around the neck, measured how much cloth would be needed for the job.

"I shall embroider for you the most wonderful collar, you will see," she whispered into his ear. "A collar of green, as bright as fresh birch leaves in summer, against a yellow background."

Inside the shop, adults were busy purchasing items for their children. Pitlor received two silk-cut dresses, one from her Uncle Volodya and another from her Uncle Ilya. Grandmother bought beads, and mother purchased a piece of cloth to make a garment for herself, and, of course, the collar for Longlegs.

"Anka! Buy me things!" Pitlor squealed, tugging at her mother's dress.

Not knowing what "things" her daughter wanted, her mother grabbed a mixture of various sweets. Having noticed the beads, she bought her daughter a beautiful matching red necklace.

"*At lankhalayam mampash!* I don't want candies!" someone cried. It was the funny boy, Peter.

Pitlor didn't know any Russian yet, so could not understand what was said, but she had already drawn more attention than she wished for. In confusion, she hid under her mother's wide dress. As for the young elk, it pushed its long, pretty face into a bag of goods as soon as it got a chance. Finding sweets, he started to devour without distinction whatever was in the bag. Chasing the candy-lover from the store, the salesman hid his merchandise behind the counter.

"You, girl, come here and show me what you think you need!" the salesman called to Pitlor.

Complete silence fell in the shop, as still clutching her mother's dress, Pitlor moved towards the counter. The unknown "things" she spotted there included a smoked sausage, which she grabbed and sniffed. The customers chortled.

"So much for things", they joked, the salesman laughing in chorus with them, as the girl let go of her mother's dress and slipped out of the shop.

Outside, she found Sorjyokhan and the young elk, each of whom still expected to receive presents. On the way out she had already nibbled a piece of sausage, food which was completely unfamiliar to her, but she found its taste all the more pleasant for it. Breaking off a slice, she gave it to Longlegs, who snaffled it and asked for more. By the time the human cubs and the forest cub reached home, there was nothing left of the sausage.

Back at the store, the adults lingered. Since all of the village's population was gathered there, they had lots to talk about. Whilst waiting for the adults to arrive, the children soon felt discomfort in their stomachs. They sat propped against the stove, feeling terribly thirsty. From time to time, Pitlor filled a bucket of water and drank from it. The young elk also came up to the bucket, thrust its entire handsome face into it and emptied it completely. Suffering dreadfully, Pitlor lay down on the cool grass, the young elk curling up at her feet. The earth felt refreshing, but the pain persisted. Shortly, the girl started to feel sick. After all, smoked sausage was not something which children were built to consume.

When the adults arrived, the children drank three entire buckets more and lay back down on the grass. Mother rushed to the paramedic who lived at the other end of the village and promised to buy "Russian panacea" in the shop. Pitlor would not have any appetite for sausage for a long time to come.

By September, the children's cousins had set off for boarding school. From now on, nobody would come to play with Pitlor and Sorjyokhan as they did during the summer holidays, since all of them were now at school.

That year, the cedars bore their juicy nuts in larger quantities than usual. Uncle Yukhur gathered them in the wood, as well as reindeer lichen for the young elk and the deer to feed on. As they would never refuse an excursion to the woods, the children went along to assist him. "Now collect what you can in the forest," uncle instructed them. "There's much work to be done. We'll have a rich harvest today. We'll not have to worry about feeding the animals, since here they don't depend on the bread and the fish we humans prepare, but can live on their favourite food, namely reindeer lichen."

"Will Longlegs join us in the boat?" Sorjyokhan asked.

"No. He will run along with us on the bank," Uncle Yukhur replied, "and we shall go to Erapta, where the deer are grazing."

"*Ma! Met oln to aktashchla! Ma! Ma!*- Me, I want to go first to collect it! Me! Me!" the children shouted.

With this little war of words, they ran to their grandmother, who was waiting for them and gave them each a food parcel for the journey. Bags for reindeer lichen and cedar fruits were also made ready, and soon their boots were gleaming under the rays of the morning sun. In September, water had seeped back to the shore, so one could no longer run along the bank in summer footwear; but when you wear boots on this strip of land, the marshy *oozy nyasha*, you have to watch your step in order not to get stuck.

Having thus prepared for the road, carrying the food grandmother had made for them, the children headed back to their uncle. Devoted to his master like an obedient child, the young elk used all the strength in his long legs to push forward and join the party, overtaking them along the way. Uncle Yukhur moved the boat into the water and they stepped in, careful not to get mud on their boots. As they sat on the floor, their uncle started the engine and let the boat glide towards Erapta. Nervously prancing along the bank, at first the young elk had wanted to join them in the boat, but realising he could just as well follow the vessel on land, he trailed the boat from the shore

Having arrived at a spot where reindeer lichen was growing, Uncle Yukhur steered the boat towards the bank. Recognizing his birthplace and perhaps thinking the boat would leave without him, Longlegs dashed into the water and inevitably got stuck in the mud. Instead of withdrawing to the coast, he continued to move further into the river, which only made the muds grip on him worse. His legs were thin, and the bog was already up to his breast, but Longlegs continued to fight for his life, shaking his head as tears sprung from his doleful eyes. Looking up at Uncle Yukhur - who for him was both mother and father - and for Pitlor and Sorjyokhan, whom he considered brother and sister, the young elk panted, gasping for air, and soon could only move his head.

Jumping from the vessel, Uncle Yukhur ordered the children to go ashore and gather grass. Fearing for the young elk, they ripped up clumps of grass until their palms bled, Pitlor's heavy copper jewelry hindering her and jingling as it fell below her wrists. His hands full, Sorjyokhan ran towards the bank, but encumbered by her ornaments, Pitlor bent over once more, pulling long strings of grass from the ground. Her heart pounded in her chest as the young elk gasped for air. Longlegs could drown. Never mind her bleeding hands and the sharp pain which had somehow spread down to her heels; she must keep working!

"Take this and cut at the roots;" Sorjyokhan said, passing her a knife.

The girl was relieved, recalling how her grandmother cut weeds in this manner.

Having no rope to hand, Uncle Yukhur wove the grass into a thin string, like a maiden's braid. The children watched his handiwork anxiously; would this really work? Would this string of coarse grass save Longlegs?

"I made the rope stronger and thicker, lest it should cut kuran's skin," uncle explained.

Placing a thick *talnik* branch across the marsh, Yukhur walked towards the struggling animal. Dipping his hands into the marsh, he tied Longlegs under the stomach and across his front, then threw the rope to the children.

"*Muy! Sukhtalzv voyev, tat hun zhaylzv!* Pull the rope! We shall not leave our Longlegs behind!" Yukhur ordered, gladdened by his niece and nephew's love for the animal as they seized the rope and tugged with all their might.

"Not too fast or we could hurt kuran," he warned. "Don't be afraid, we shall save our baby!"

Trying to free himself from both the mud and the rope, Longlegs wrestled with amazing strength for a calf of only four months. As soon as the mud released the elk, uncle pulled him to dry land with such force that the exhausted animal could not stand. The children ran up to the mud-caked animal they loved with all their hearts, hugging him across his flanks. The kuran then sprung to his feet, forgetting who his saviours were. He still felt danger. Seeking firmer ground, he stopped a few metres closer to the trees as though he just thought of something, and shook so hard that pieces of slurry flew from his fur, hitting the children and their uncle. They all laughed loudly, relieved that everything had worked out.

After a short rest, the travellers went to gather cedar fruits and reindeer lichen. The young elk would need to eat as well after all that had occurred. Yukhur took a large basket woven from thick reed and forced the rich fruit from the dense branches by beating the cedar trunks with a stick. Within seconds, a shower of fruit fell. Playing with the young elk, all of them still coated in mud, Pitlor and Sorjyokhan started to gather the fruit with great enthusiasm whilst Yukhur collected reindeer lichen.

"I have the biggest nut!"

"But I have more!" the children exclaimed joyfully.

Not understanding the attraction of these tasteless fruits, the young elk sniffed at them with indifference. Collecting a large heap, Sorjyokhan and Pitlor placed them in the basket. Finding them was not so simple, as most of those that fell became hidden in the long grass or rolled under bushes. Feeling rather tired, the children sat down and started peeling the resinous skins from the nuts. Soon the wood was filled with the oily aroma of them. From time to time, Uncle Yukhur could be heard slamming a trunk. The echo resounded through the forest and the children felt reassured, knowing that he was nearby. Probably still remembering the fearful adventure he had endured, Longlegs lay down near the children, curled up and fell into an uneasy sleep. He looked a strange sight with clay, leaves, grass and cedar nut skins stuck to his fur. Fitfully woken by the animated exclamations of the children, he raised his head, but then hid it again between his forelegs.

Shortly, uncle appeared from the woods with three bags hanging over his shoulder, two filled with reindeer lichen and the other with cedar nuts.

"Why is our basket almost empty while we searched everywhere for nuts?" the children asked in disappointment.

"My dear friends, you can collect lots of fruit from a single tree, but as you can see, I collected them from five trees. I need a rest, and at home it's teatime now."

Yukhur unwrapped the food grandmother had packed for them. The nuts had been nourishing enough, but who would refuse something more substantial? Devouring the supplies, the children give a slice of bread to Longlegs, who chewed upon it reticently. The mud bath had done him little good, and he was still in a state of shock.

That evening at supper, Uncle Yukhur broached a difficult subject.

"In the morning, we should all get up a bit earlier," he said. "We shall take Longlegs to the woods."

"To the woods?" the children exclaimed. "Why take Longlegs to the woods? He'll get lost out there!"

"The forest is our young elk's home," Uncle Yukhur answered quietly. "It's where his mother lives, waiting for her little son to return. Our kuran is growing up now, getting stronger and more independent. Come fall his mother will return in search of grounds to graze upon during the winter, and that's where they will meet."

"And who shall we play with then?" Pitlor asked in distress.

"He'll be better off in the forest than among people," Yukhur said, unwilling to answer any more questions.

Yukhur went outside. His reason told him that an elk has to live in the woods, but he also felt affection for the animal as if it were a relative. Like his niece and nephew, he felt a childlike urge not to give way to reason, but to let his emotions prevail. He was also afraid, however, that if the calf got too used to life amongst people, it would become a stranger to the woods and might not survive upon its return. After all, although he was born in the wild, the forest had already become unknown terrain to him.

"Our young elk grows and matures by the day," Yukhur's old mother said to the children. "Very soon he will want to meet others of his kind. He will not be able to live among people forever. That is why we must take Longlegs back to his home."

After their meal, trying to cheer up the gloomy children, grandmother told Pitlor to find the green collar.

"Longlegs will need his collar," she said. "There are always lots of hunters around, and if they see the collar they won't harm your friend."

"I shall embroider yellow marks on it," Pitlor said, still filled with grief, "like autumn leaves on the road."

The children then inundated their grandmother with all the questions they wanted answered.

"Where in the woods will Longlegs live?"

"At his home, where his mother lives. She's been waiting for him for so long now."

"And what kind of house is that?"

"A house," unanki paused, "a house made of birch, clad in white *yagushka*[15] and *mailtsa*[16] and topped with branches from the cedar tree to protect him from the wind and rain."

"What a wonderful house," Pitlor said, with a sigh of relief, "like a handsome estate decorated with tree branches. And where will he sleep?"

"His mother will make him a bed of soft green grass, with a pillow of Labrador tea leaves. When he goes to sleep on such a pillow, he is bound to dream about my grandchildren!"

"Well, if his mother has prepared such a delightful home, then we should take him to the wood," Pitlor

15 *Woman's coat made from the skin of a fawn*

16 *Man's coat made from reindeer fur*

decided, though still struggling with having to separate from her friend.

"Well said," grandmother concurred. "He must miss his mother very much, and in the woods he will make friends of his own kind. After all, if he talks to you, you don't understand, and he doesn't comprehend any human language. Longlegs also needs to talk and share his pleasures with his friends and family."

To make the collar, grandmother took her oldest piece of cloth she had which could easily be torn, even by the hands of children. The sooner the collar breaks and kuran loses our gift, the better it will be for him, she thought. Wearing it will make it harder for him to breathe, for as he grows the collar will become too small for him.

When they arose at sunrise, the grass, the trees and even the blades of the oars were covered with dew, which shone like tears, casting a silver gleam. The children stepped carefully on the ground in order not to damage the blanket of dew, but the young elk trampled on hundreds of dewdrops and rolled over on the grass. On the river bank, Longlegs was carried into the boat, his legs tied together so he could not jump out. Pitlor and Sorjyokhan became covered in mud by the young animal, sweat pouring down his face as he struggled to get free.

"Do not be afraid; we are bringing you to your mother. She will recognise you at once and take you to your own home," the children reassured him, comforting themselves in the process.

Soon they were laughing, though, the calf tickling their cheeks with his long tongue. Lifting in the sky, the sun shone bright and reflected on the water. At the edge of the forest, Yukhur moored the vessel, and together with the children he lifted the kuran out. He had returned to his natural habitat.

Approaching a mountain ash tree, Longlegs sniffed at its coloured berries, upon which a shower of icy beads fell onto his snout. Frightened, he ran back to the children. Shortly curious once more, he then spotted the large petals of a burdock covered with dewdrops, and curled his lips wishing to drink since the silver droplets were falling into a hollow. His thirst sated, the young elk was pacified.

"In the woods, the hollows collect water even though the dewdrops are small," Sorjyokhan told Pitlor. "Grandmother said that there are lots of streams in the woods, and when water from a *soym*[17] flows into the Ob, the river refreshes itself," he whispered, trying not to disturb the forest's early morning silence. "And I know that the leaves will soon fall from the trees."

Affected by the cold, the birches were already turning yellow.

"Aka, why is there so much water? It was not like this the other day," Pitlor asked curiously.

"This is *yik*: night water. During the night, blind Grandfather Fog wanders confused dressed in a large white parka coat and leaves this moisture lying all around. That's

17 *A small river flowing from a spring*

why it's wet here now, and will be until the afternoon sun comes and drinks up all the dew."

Approaching an ailing birch tree, Longlegs stuck out his tongue in search of something to eat, icy droplets falling onto his head once more.

Uncle Yukhur tied the elk to a tree with a cord. Ordering the children to stay in the boat, he vanished into the woods. The day advanced, the low autumn sun sucking the ground dry. With their uncle out of sight, the children occupied themselves with the tiny fish that merrily jumped from the water to catch the breadcrumbs that Pitlor and Sorjyokhan cast them. Sensing food, the small schchurogaychik fish floated near the surface. When the children splashed the water with the oars they scattered, but soon reemerged again.

It was thus that Yukhur found them, and without uttering a word started the engine. Observing his gloomy countenance, the boy and the girl wanted to ask questions, but they knew that their kind uncle would remain hushed until he felt like speaking. After he had piloted the vessel almost a kilometre from the bank, all of a sudden the children began to shout.

"Kuran, our Longlegs! Look, uncle!"

Bounding along the bank, sometimes slipping on the mud, there was the young elk.

"He did not want to live with his mother," the children squealed in delight. "He wants to continue living with us!"

That day, Longlegs was brought back home again.

Under the Constellation of the Elk

Pitlor was lying in bed, unable to even lift her head. She was so sick that she had no appetite whatsoever. Outside the frost was drawing fancifully on her window. Somewhere, the sun was resting, sleeping peacefully. Red-faced Nye-Imi does not like the cold when there is nowhere to shelter. Frozen under a three-metre thick layer of ice and covered by in a white blanket of wooly snow, the broad Ob River was slumbering as well. Sometimes, on clear days, Nye-Imi would briefly wake and glance at the streets to see how people were doing and whether they too were frozen. Seeing the smoke coming from the chimneys, she would sigh serenely, returning with red cheeks to her own golden shelter.

The girl wanted to reach out the window, but lacked the strength to do so. Her mother and grandmother had put so many sweets near the bed; if she were healthy she'd have eaten them all by now, but with no appetite for them they remained where they were, gathering dust. From time to time, her mother would give her some medicine using a trick the girl knew all too well. Turning her back on her daughter, she would pour a spoonful of medicine from a flask and mix it with compote.

"Look, I brought you delicious compote, with apples and sweet berries that come from the warm lands where they grow on the trees," she would say. "Drink some, it's quite delicious."

Pitlor would imagine a large number of cans filled with compote dangling from the branches of trees. Quite why the branches didn't break under their weight, she couldn't tell.

"Anka! Give me a bucket of cold water made from snow," she asked her mother.

"I cannot do that, or you will surely be taken to the hospital," her mother replied.

"Then give me a piece of frozen milk; I need something cold!"

"I can't, my Pitlor. The doctors will say I made you worse."

Grandmother entered the house. She was followed by the young elk, moving clumsily and slipping on the coloured tiles. Having reached the living room, he sat on the ground, but recognising the girl lying under a pile of blankets, he rose to his feet and came to the patient's bedside.

"Now here comes my voracious companion," Pitlor whispered, "out for my sweets and my compote, not intending to leave anything for me."

The young elk sniffed at the jars of compote on the shelf, then licked his little hostess's hand. Something in it made him feel good, and he kept licking her palm.

"All right, I shall give you half of what you like, and you will find it truly tasty," she said.

The young elk glanced at the door. When it opened, he would have his chance to escape onto the street. This was the time of day when Uncle Yukhur and Sorjyokhan would return home after their horses had pulled fresh drinking water out of the river through a hole in the ice. Pitlor remembered the day Sorjyokhan had mounted a horse for the first time. Usually, children learnt how to mount a horse by leading it to a stable, climbing onto the roof and jumping onto the horse's back from there. Sometimes, if the horse felt he could not tolerate it and bolted, children would fly into the air and end up face down in the snow. In her mind, Uncle Yukhur placed Pitlor on a horse, while Sorjyokhan climbed onto the roof of the stable. It was not a simple thing, but he wouldn't give up.

One day, Yukhur had arrived back early from Erapta with three sled deer for his brother, who had a herd in the summer pastures of the polar Ural Mountains. Yukhur had helped his brother to find a spot rich with reindeer lichen. Upon their horses, the children rode off over the hills, but having no saddle, Pitlor found it hard to stay upon her steed. While the horse was galloping, she was thrown over its head and landed at its feet. The horse, in turn, jumped over the girl without touching her with a single hoof. Sorjyokhan laughed and Pitlor, feeling humiliated,ran after the horse in the direction of an ice hole.

"You never caught up with me, and now it seems you can't even sit on a horse!" the boy jeered.

Pitlor brooded in silence. Unable to mount the horse, she climbed back up the slope, whilst Sorjyokhan sat proudly upon his colt. Cantering alongside, Longlegs nudged the girl playfully, but only managed to knock her down in the snow. Climbing back to her feet, Pitlor pushed the calf aside, but he was just glad of the attention. Shouting at the young elk, Pitlor started to cry loudly and desperately.

"Go away, leave me alone. You humiliated me, making me fall into the snow," she cried, scowling at the innocent animal.

Without waiting for the screaming girl to calm down, Longlegs scurried back to the house.

Later, he watched the girl bending over a warming bowl of cabbage soup. He felt sorry to have upset her and realised that without her to play with, life would be very dull. When she finished the soup, Pitlor took a coat of *yagushka* fur and placed it on herself to keep out the chill. The moon had been shining brightly for two weeks now, and a certain clutch of stars had caught her eye. The sky was filled with numberless stars, shining like jewels. Drawing an imaginary line with her finger, she marked the sign of the elk, about which grandmother had often told her.

"I offended the poor animal," she said to herself, "and here is his star sign looking down on me, probably thinking that I've acted badly; but he did kick me, after all."

Staring up at the stars, she thought to weave them together into a silver brooch for her mother.

Jewellery was rarely brought to the village shop, though ladies liked it very much. Imagining gifting the shining stars to her mother, Pitlor smiled, rose to her feet, wiped the remnants of her tears from her face and shook the snow off her yagushka.

Returning from her reverie on this dark winter evening, Pitlor noticed the thin crescent moon radiating a halo of light about the house. Sorjyokhan will be very happy if he managed to mount the horse today, and here I am so ill, she pondered bitterly.

As Yukhur opened the door opened, Longlegs scampered from the house, his hooves thundering in the direction of the stables.

Having entered the house with Yukhur, Sorjyokhan was playing listlessly with his toys.

"You want gingerbread?" he asked his sister.

Still with no appetite, Pitlor shook her head.

"You can bring me a bucket of ice cold water made from snow," she said, noticing that her mother had left to milk the cows.

Glad to be of assistance, Sorjyokhan brought a bucket of water so cold it would freeze your teeth. Seeing that his sister could not raise her head, he took a spoon and filled it with water mixed with medicine. It was delicious and Pitlor would have drunk it all, but then mother came in. On seeing her son with the spoon, she pushed him aside. No one could tell whether it had been because of the water, but the next day Pitlor's fever broke and she devoured all of the compotes.

The Music of Narasjyuka Forest

In the morning, they were to set out for the woods to collect reindeer moss from the fir trees.

They had to go to sleep early, and Uncle Yukhur led by example, spreading out his bed. The children turned in reluctantly. Naturally, they wanted to walk in the forest, but they didn't want to go to bed.

In the springtime, the woods are particularly beautiful. The sun shines on the glades and the trees prepare for summer. The needled cedar branches gaining in strength as their colour changes from undefined and dull into brilliant emerald, their crests reach out towards the sun. The birches dress in their alluring white mantles. Which adornment is the most beautiful and will arrest the attention of visitors?

The ancient cedars silently stare at the fashionably dressed women preparing for the short summer. Squirrels, martens, *kedruvkiy* and other birds are already searching for food, collecting provisions for the long winter, for the summer will soon be no more than a memory. The larch trees, having cast off the snow that kept them warm, stretch their soft needles. They stand there, proud and serene. It is not for nothing that the Khanty only allow men to touch their bark.

Brushy old fir trees overgrown with grey moss look from under their hairy eyebrows, like storytellers. They are waiting for the deer and the elks to strip them off their winter costumes. Then there are the ancient fir trees all covered in moss, which grows not only on their branches, but also on their trunks which date back to time immemorial.

The sun's rays reached everywhere on this morning. Even the sleepy mice came from their nests and scuttled through the trees looking for fresh food. The forest was filled with birdsong, resounding like the strings of the old *naras-jyuka*[18], and merrily welcoming the beams of light.

The inhabitants of the forest had waited so long through the fierce, icy cold for gentle Nye-Imi.

Amidst this cheerful chorus, however, there was a doleful sound emanating from someone who was not scared of the dark polar nights. As the young elk approached the owl, he raised his long ears, unfamiliar as he was with the woods and its inhabitants. Annoyed by the racket that came with spring, preventing him from sleeping after a long night of hunting, the owl placed his wing over his head. To him it didn't matter whether it was summer or winter; his thick feathered fur protected him from the frost.

---

18 *A stringed instrument played by plucking*

The moss collectors had placed large hunting skis on their feet, in which they moved with ease across the crust of biting snow to the tune of the strings of the narasjyuka. Uncle Yukhur had skis covered with skin which rustled in the snow.

"*Shchyurk-shchyurk*", he cried, mimicking the sound made by the children's footwear.

Slipping time and again on the snow, Longlegs banged his hooves, but Yukhur couldn't provide him with four skis!

At first, the visitors gathered only the moss growing on the lower branches. Collecting it alongside them, for Longlegs the moss under the gentle beams of the spring sun was a delicacy like no other. Sometimes he unintentionally pushed the children into the snow, and though he was only playing, the children shouted at him in protest. Having harvested all the moss from the lower branches, Pitlor begged to be lifted to higher ones.

"I cannot climb those branches," she said. "Aka, help me up there, please; this long-legged creature has bothered me enough!"

Yukhur placed the girl upon a strong branch and handed her a bag. Watching the girl, the calf snapped at a lower branch - possibly to eat more, or perhaps to climb after her – but the result was that the branch supporting Pitlor started to shake and she screamed in fear.

"Get away from me! Go to aka, he has the longest and tastiest bits! Mine are short and completely tasteless! You see, I cannot stomach a single bit of it! Phew!" she added, spitting out a piece of bitter moss, though she knew that to the elk it tasted quite different.

As she expected, though, he wouldn't move away from the tree. The more his hospitable little friend struggled, the more he stretched his neck. Maybe he was trying to get hold of her feet or to snatch a bunch of kysok, or perhaps he was afraid that she might fall. Leaving the branches shaking unsteadily, the young elk ran off as though looking for someone else to disturb, and the girl plopped down into a snowdrift.

"*Mang talt ate!* My bag is empty, so do not disturb me!" a voice deep in the woods howled. "And get off my ski! Yaa!"

A cracking noise rang out, and with tears in his eyes Sorjyokhan emerged, trying to fit back together the pieces of a ski.

"You broke my ski!" he cried, slapping the young elk on the back. "How will I get home on

just one ski?" he asked his uncle, who had appeared from between the trees.

"We shall get home somehow," Yukhur consoled him. "One ski is not the end of the world.

Uncle Yukhur threw two bags full of moss over his shoulder, the children staring at him in amazement. When did he manage to collect all that? Between the pair of them, the children hadnot even half a bag.

And so the foragers headed for home.

"From now on, Longlegs will likely eat the food that's appropriate for him," aka said. "He'll have no wish for salted bread; he'll not be able to stomach it. Moss is his dish. All elks chew moss and tree crusts during winter."

And so a second year passed with the young elk sticking around, strengthening Uncle Yukhur's belief in the forces of nature.

In April, when spring was in full bloom, early one morning Yukhur left together with his long-legged friend for the village of Vulykurt. He returned alone late at night, brooding and exhausted. Grandmother moved busily around her son as he ate his supper in dumb silence. The children were gloomy too, wondering what had happened to Longlegs, but taking care so as not to upset their uncle, who sipped his tea noisily and would not make eye contact with anyone.

"Sweep the tears from your eyes, and go into the street to play!" Grandmother exclaimed,

glancing through the window and throwing her arms in the air. "Kuran the brave roamer has returned to base!"

Uncle's face brightened as the children burst onto the street. Tired, the young elk rolled over amongst the needles. Profoundly happy that he'd found his way home, he pushed his handsome face into the children's palms.

***

Today, Uncle Yukhur sat around the house, tired and depressed. It was clear to see that his strength had completely deserted him. In the evening, Sorjyokhan arrived on a *kaldanke*[19] from Saimaa. He left the boat and climbed the hill towards the heavy wooden house where the adults were gathered. When he entered, they didn't raise their eyes. Pitlor quickly understood everything. She perceived that Longlegs had died and had been buried in the woods. A powerful shot of grief ran through her, preventing her from breathing.

Grandmother expressed her support for them in silence. She understood that her son had lost his heart to a forest animal, and how her grandchildren had lost the company of such a merry and tender animal. A long stillness followed, during which tears fell from the children's eyes and Uncle Yukhur tried to pull himself together as a real man of the north would.

"But why?" Pitlor cried from the very pit of her tormented soul. "Why was he lost to us?"

At last, Uncle Yukhur, who hadn't uttered a word all day started to talk in an attempt to answer the children's questions.

"I should never have brought the kuran to a human dwelling," he said mournfully. "I should have left him with his broken leg on the shore, and his mother would have come back. After all, the wood was his home and he would

19 *Small fishing boat*

have managed to survive. A forest animal should live in the forest! Each living creature should live where he comes from and where he belongs.

Everything has been wrong – so terribly wrong!"

Epilogue

Life runs by in a hurry, heading in one direction or another, and so does mine, leaving me with no time. My native, majestic Blue River rushes its water to the cold Kara Sea, never resting.

Cycles will be broken and things disappear, so everything perishes. This is just nature taking its course. As for my life, it never stopped rushing past for a moment from the very beginning. It has brought me sparkling memories and profound impressions which are impossible to forget.

Two years I spent with the small wild elk: shy, harmless and impossible to find fault with, just giving of its love. The kuran was fundamental to the formation of my personality, so my words can but fail to express my true thoughts and feelings. The world I shared with this wild animal and the lessons my grandmother taught me told me everything about the worldview of the Khanty people.

The spontaneity of those times put me on the path to respect for the elderly and love for animals, and helped me to realise how simple it is to do good deeds. This education was of a spiritual kind, helping me to fully perceive the world around me. A storehouse of knowledge with regard to our traditions, my grandmother taught me the wisdom passed down from our ancestors. She warmed us all with the compassion in her soul. She helped us to comprehend the harmony in nature, and to communicate with our lifeblood, the River Ob. I began to take an interest to Xi - the personification of nature as perceived by our people - and started to study this. To my aid came the insight of my unanki, my senior mother, whose life experience proved of immense value. A youngster with a fair, honest and reliable disposition is sensitive to such an education.

My Uncle was also worthy of great respect for the help and protection he afforded us. As for Longlegs, merry and strange, he drew us children towards him. This is why the time spent in the company of a wild animal, to my mind, is more important than what we studied at school in front of a computer.

Today, people talk about ecological education, but in reality, this reveals a shortcoming. For us, there was never any need to be taught about interaction with nature: we simply lived in that world, and for us everything was natural. Probably, we were just lucky, and therefore I couldn't remain silent about out long-legged friend, and refrain from telling you about what continues to capture my heart. About the dear people and the beloved, speechless young elk, who couldn't express his tenderness and love in words, but whom I will always remember. About everything I loved, and all who fostered me. None of them are anywhere near me these days: my grandmother, my aka, my brother Sorjyokhan or the young elk, so it is up to me to tell how a little wild animal taught us how to love. About a grandmother who cared so much about her three children; after all, Uncle Yukhur always remained a child to her. Aka, our image of perfection, the serious adult and man of the world, he too was a boy in the company of this animal. We children were able to forget our sorrows, but the pain hit our uncle more keenly.

These are the experiences which helped shape my personality. I will never hit an animal, cut a tree or pick a flower without good reason. If I sense a young elk in the woods, I'll look for a pair of eyes deep in the thicket, there in the wilds, hoping for an encounter. One thing I know for sure: my dear friend will always be in my heart.

Восты йиӈкпи
Ун Ас панан

HERTFORDSHIRE PRESS

Хув кураŋ вой нёпие

Щи нупт хатљ Питљор эвие, самљ паканман, ун акайљ хот пеља туп љаљтман, сора нёхаммаљ онтасан, хухаљман манс. Хатљ кутапан, каш верты хотн няврэмат ураŋан кина аиљыты вер ус, щи ураŋан там пелак курта љув ёхтас. Няврэмат ељта љувеља уваљтсат:

– Кураŋ войн щи арат мампащ љэс па, хаљты хорпељ…

Щутщаты хатаљан ивевн каш верты хота рущт ёхтыљысат, кураŋ вой эљты уятман, ивевн патн каман хорпи мавŋ љэтот, муй мавнянь аљэмиљат. Кураŋ вой пошхие, няврэм юкана, кашŋ хоят эљты мав няварaљ. Муй мойљапсайн мешапља, муйн маља, щитљ мохты ёхи љухљапљаљљы, ёхи љавемаљљы. Щи хатљ шек ар хоят ёхтыљыяс, тэљые мавŋ љэтотан тутљыса…

Ун акайљ ов пелак пуŋаљан, Питљор эвие ромат хухаљмаљ эљты йи лота љоямтас. Юхур акайљ, воиељ хонљ эљты вощхиман опсас. Кураŋ вой пошхиељ хонљ нох пуксапмаљ. Ай эвие вана аиљтыена хатаљтыяс, курŋаљаљ вољљы щёмљы йистан… Акайљ пуŋља ванашак ювман, љувељ љаŋкар пелак нёхтасљы, нэмољты эљты ант инщасман, веншаљ пеља аŋкармас. Ай акайљ нохљы апщељ пеља аŋкармас, сэмљаљ вољљы кашаŋ хоят щирн, сэм йиŋк шуван, паљаŋ иты лап тувамат. Щиŋанща яљпа охаљ иљ эсаљсаљљы, воиељ вощхиман. Охаљ иљ эсаљман кемн сэмьйиŋкљаљ иљ ховемасат, кураŋ вой нох пуксамтам хонаља. Щи онтасан воиељ нёхайљ нох таратас. Ищи матты кущайљ сэмьйиӈк щалян, сэмљаљ шукан пелки пушмасљы, щаљта яљпа лап матсат. Хув курыиљаљ йи пуш па таратсат. Питљор эвие утљас, ай акайљ иса няхман, тумтак вантты, воиељ па иса хухатљыты кеша вантыман, Питљор эвие самљ пакнас. Ёшииљаљ машкия катаљмаман, ељ хухаљмас, щи љоват акайљ щаля йис. Юхур акайљ ивевн няхмаӈ, каркам ху, вољљы иса вевтам хорпия ювмаљ. Веншаљ, шук туты хоятат иты, питыя сухтатмаљ, ищи матты нумасаљ, ма љуљн парљам, туп воем ант ат хаљаљ. Щи љоват нопсаљ шакмаљ па, апщиељ пеља па аты аӈкармияс, хољта пеља тумељ хухаљман манс. Лум љыпийн энмаљтам воиељ хонљ эљты вощхисљы, щёрљаљ ай юх нувиенан ким караљаман щиты щи хащс. Хољљамаљ антом, самљ хошиман войљ хон таӈартысљы, мосаӈ хољна тумтакљаљ. Љув кимет номасан ищипа ям пеља нумасас, туп кураӈ отыељ па аты нёхљас. Апщиељ па самљ паканман, сора, такан, вот иты хухаљман, ныкљы, сойм пеља наварман манс. Вош хуват манам юшљ аты моштасљы, курљаљн ант нумман туса. Муй арат хот, муй арат хоят камн ус, аты шияљасљы. Хойн ищмиса, ант хуљтсаљљы. Самиељ вурн пошса, акайљ щаљ онтасан. Ешавуљ сойм унта љоӈемас. Там унт юшљ хуват шек куш паљман, хурыман яӈхас ељпи, ин па аты шияљасљы, хољта пеља курљаљн туља. Сэмьйиӈкљаљ туп ивевн этман, лакки рыйяљман ох пушхаљан ёваљмияс. Пощтуљ Питљор эвие ељпи туп кетмиља, мохты хољљап сура ниӈхарљаты питщаљ. Ин па таљ сэмьйиӈкљаљ туп раниљат. Хољљаты шийљ антом, иса машья. Щи љоват самиељ хошияс кат пиљаљ эљты. Войљ хоты хаљам щирљ вантмаљ антом, акайљ сэмьйиӈки вешљ онтасан пакнас. Щимащ юраӈ, ям хоятыељн мољхатљ щи, няхмаӈ, увман Питљор эвие ёша нох аљэмиљљы, нохљы ювтыљыман, Турам пеља. Щаљта няхман, каш верман ёхљы катљапљаљљы. Ин па акайљ хољљаљ. Хоты ун хоят поякты? Питљор эвие хољна ат уятаљ.

Покщат шоппи навармиман, сопекљаља йиӈк ант ат амарматы ураӈан, Питљор эвие щи кутн сойм потам йиӈка иљ ваклaмтас, иљ ракнас. Торнан, ваншиян лап энмам покщ ай машкиељан такан рэскасљы:

– Хом поталы! Наӈ љуљн лакки ат лосапсан.

Щи ясаӈљаљ юпиян веншаљ ваншаӈ покщ љыпия ханятсаљљы. Сыяӈа па самљ хошиман такан хољљаты питс. Унт сойм йиӈк юш лап омасмаљ онтасан, йиŋкаљ љув пуŋљаљан акмас. Ешавуљ роммамаљ юпиян, сэмьйиŋкљаљ нох мухтасљы па, нох љоямтас. Соям йиŋкаљ ныкљы ховемас, Ун Асљ пеља тэрмаљаман, ай эвие холљап сурљаљ патн тувман. Питљор эвие сойм папелка покщат эљты пурантыман, навармас. Сопекљаљ эљты йиŋкљаљ иљ шошемас, морам сохљаљ йиŋк эљты нох пащартсаљљы. Аяљтыена, па ат тэрмаљаман, ёхи шушмас. Самљ еша роммас.

Щи кат таљ ељпи, ущ ёхатты тыљащан Юхур акайљ, вељщи Ас ноптам юпиян, холљап омасты манас. Сорт хуљ муй мевты холљап љэщатас, посаљн олљаŋ хуљ ураŋан холљап омасты вераљ ус. Щи тови љув яљап мотор љутас. Каркама вой вељмаљ ураŋан ун совхоз куща икељн, Георгий Яковлевич Саенко љухсаљн ишк нэпекан муйн мойљаса. Щи митн холљна, курта тувам, сора яŋхты мотор љувеља тыныса. Щи онтасан ин љув такан яŋхты хопаљн, ай вот рув ещаљт мотораљн каш щирн манс. Хопаља љэљтаљ ељпиян, аŋкељн эљты тайман, шаващман, ястаса:

– Похие! Вељщи хопена љэљљан, охсохљан, веншен Ас йиŋкан лёхеми. Тумтак ат яŋхљан. Сора яŋхты, кумрэматы мотор муй ям онтас тайљ. Йиŋк Урр Именан ат шавиљайн. Юхур шек аŋкељ пеља хуљатман ус. Намн охсохљаљ, веншаљ йиŋкан лёхемасљы, ястаман:

– Ущ вой, поть, поть, поть! Љор вой, поть, поть, поть!

Ин сора яŋхты хопаљн вот рув ещаљт манман опсас. Нуй куващ милаљ холљна охаљ эљты вотн иљ пољэмаса. Шек потраŋ Юхур антом ус, хоятат пеља вещкат па ром ус. Ляватты верљ антом ус, ром щирн мохет пеља потартыман ус. Щи онтасан мохет ям щирн љув пиљаљн потарпсат, ям номас хуват усат. Ин па лавм хорпи сэмљаљн посљ вутатн вантман омастаљ эљты, еŋк шупат пуŋаљан, туса йиран манман, ёхљы пеља юшљ вусљы, холпаљ омассаљљы. Мољхатљ, ун овас вотљ роммас. Етн, посљаљ муйн еŋкаљ эљты таљамас. Щи ељпи хоты хуљам хатљ кеша Овас вотљ Ялань ики иты якас, таранљыяс. Еŋкљаљ каман щира ий эљты вощкиман ешащас. Еŋкљаљ хопематаљ кемн, ворс па сый. Юхат, варсат муйн патн Ас йиŋка нярэмаман таранљыяс. Ищи матты Ялань икељ мољты нељты љаŋхаса, пулэматы љэтот каншман. Иљампа Ялань икељ мољты мощатмаљ. Таљ, ищки вот рувљ мољхатљ роммас. Ин там хатљ па наяŋ, ям хатљ. Кармас кутн Юхур кураŋ вой шияљас. Вана ёхатмаљн, кураӈ войљ, хоят эљты паљтамаман, посљ папелка ущман манс. Варс кутн па Юхур ай нёпие шияљас. Аӈкељ таӈха нyаврэмиељ хоят ёша митаљасљы, љув юрљ ант тараммаљ ураӈан. Хопаљн Юхур вана љоваљмас, ай войљ хоща. Варс кут эљты хайм отыељ нох љарпитсаљљы, па ныкљышак поткасљы:

– Я, ята, мана, мана аӈкен юпиян! Муя ант манљан. Ий пуш па ёшаљ йиӈка лукемасљы, войљ маљысыман. Щитаљн, нёпиељ курљ шукатмаљ, щи онтасан, аӈкељ юпиян ант вертмаљ манты. Хоты верты, Юхур, потам йинк эљты аљ тарыты воиељ хоп љыпия нох сухтасљы. Ай отыељ, нyаврэм иты хуљатман, хоят ёша ищи матты йиӈк хуват љув хощайљ ущмас. Хоят ёшн вољљы иса роммас, шитама йис. Аяљтыена нёпиељ хоп љыпия потсаљљы, эљты ерт сохн лап лаксаљљы, еша ат хошмаљтыяљ. Войљ лакман, хоят пиљн ищи матты потартантыяс:

– Потам йиӈкан Аса ант нопатсайн, щит ям. Љыљӈа хащсан, муй па мосаљ. Курыен хоты муӈ тумтакљаљэв. Љухсат муйн уятљан. Аӈкен хоты манс. Хольща ин мин љувељ каншљэмн? Матты мува манс, хольща уятљэмн. Минэмн хун па нётљ. – Щитаљн юраӈ мотораљ сухтасљы па, куртаља, ёхљы пеља юшљ вуcљы.

Юхур хиљэӈаљљаљ, наяӈ љуӈ хатаљан, хатљ хуват каман ёнтман ешащсатан. Ёнтман, аты шияљасљан, хун ай акайн сора яӈхты хопаљн вуты хойс. Хот пушас пуӈљаља ёхатмаљ кемн туп сэмљан ромат љув пељайљ ющатсат. Акайн амуй воие апаљмамаљ. Щи љоват хув кураӈ воие, курљаљ љув сахатэљ иљта ропсэмиман ёвљасљат. Щимащ вер шияљаман, ещаљт навармастан. Љын хољна ант вантыям хув кураӈ войн. Вана ёхтапман кемн, войн, ох пушхиељ паљтамаман куш хољта тэваљты питсаљљы, акайн ёш пата. Юхурн таканшак мевљаљ пуӈља войљ апаљмасљы, роматман. Па мохты, ант љойљыман, нyаврэмат пуӈаљ эљты машьяйн шушмас. Нyаврэмӈан нэмољты ант инщасман, акайн пуӈаљан ант вантам воие пеља аӈкармиман, ищи роммаман шушмастан:

– Амуй воие? Љов хорпи вољљы антом, щи куш сохљ вурты. Курљаљ хувт. Шаншаљ мормаӈ. Анта, љов хорпи яна антом. Акайн машья, нях вешн шушаљ. Нyаврэмӈан ищи, инщматы щирн антом, ай тэљн щиты утаљтаман уљљатан, ун хоят љув ястаљ, муй мосаљ ястаты. Щишн љављасман ваныенан вой пеља вантыман щи шушсатан. Аяљтыена, рома, нёпиељ мува понмаљ юпиян, Юхур няхман ястас:

– Унаŋкан хоща хухатљыятан, хошам, эсмаŋ мисьйиŋк кеван вохатн.

– Унаŋки! Унаŋки! – сыяŋа увман нячрэмŋан хухаљман матсатан унаŋкан хоща.

– Акаеман хув кураŋ вой ахольща тувмаљ, ай мисљаман эсмаŋ мисьйиŋки кеван вохас!

Унаŋкан, ищи матты муй иса уятман, ун кеванаља мисьйиŋк шай понас. Яљап мисьйиŋк етн туп пусља. Љув хоты похиељ ёхатмаљ кемн мохты шияљасљы, муй вой пиљн тумељ ёхтас. Вељщи хун ханты хоят ай вой мощатыяс. Мет шопаŋ товийн, вељщи сэма питты войт, курљаљ ки курљаљ шукатљаљљаљ, ёшљаљ ки ёшљаљ. Похиељ вой пеља, хоят пеља щаляŋ, иса нётапљаљљы. Аŋкиељ муйн иса щалитман тайљаљљы. Ун ими мисьйиŋки кеванљ миймаљ юпиян, мисьйиŋк кев путаља шошемас, па кур љоŋљаља каvартты омассаљљы.

Питљор эвие, уртыељ Сорљёхан похие пиљн, ёхљы ёхатман кемн, ин ант вантам воие, хув кураљ хоща акаянан кељн сохаљ тохи ярам. Апщеŋаљаљ эљты кеванаљ вус, войљ мисьйиŋкан инщаљтаты питсаљљы. Тумељ ољаŋан охаљ сараљаты питсаљљы, кеванаљ ељ поткаљљы, нячрэмŋан эљты паљман, ий сэм пелакан иса љын пељайн аŋкармияљ. Нумасаљ таŋха, аљт па вељљаям там мољты ант вантыям кураŋ ёшаŋ отŋанан. Юхур кат хуљам мисьйиŋк сэм нёљ воша посэмас. Мисьйиŋк сэмт лакки рыяпсат, воие охаљн нёхтамаљ кемн. Кураŋ отыељ па такан щит эљты няхтантас. Юхур амтытљыман, щи хорпи ям воие уятмаљ ураŋан, такан няхаљтас. Хиљыеŋаљаљ ищи няхаљсатан, амтатљыман. Ай нёпие таŋха хувн ант љэс, щишн хув няљмаљн нёљаљ нёљэмасљы. Юхурн каматса сэмн па посэмаса. Ин воие аршак мисьйиŋк эљты рахаљтантыяс. Няљмаљн па щи нёљаљ нёљэмасљы. Ешавуљ, моштаман таŋха, хоятатн љапатты вуратља, анта вељты, љув кеван эсмаљ хоща нёљаљ сухтасљы. Нячрэмŋан ищи такан куш љаŋхасайтан воие љапатты, акайн љарытман, тохи куш ниншемиљтан. Туп кеванан љынан ат маса. Тови хуват љын кашаŋ хатљ ай мисљан эсмаŋ кеван эљты мисьйиŋкан љапатсаљљан. Ољаŋан хор мисн, юхат Марта мисн опсас, нэ мис пошах кеван эльты льапатсатан. Щишн шек яма хошсатан щи кемн, куш кепа хольна айӈан. Ай войӈальанан хой ишн иль паятльайтан. Ивевн ищи матты льэльы ульатан. Куш кепа хатль хуват хульам пуш ий кеван арат мисьйиӈкан льапатльальан. Льов пошахльан хольна льапатты льаӈхасайтан, туп льовльальан вана ат эсальсайтан. Щи тови льув хотэльн каман щир вой ус. Эраптайн яӈльэм пеши ин хухатльыльат. Щапа ампан ищи шек ар кутюв тайль. Ёнтты льухс тайльатан. Туп там мольты хув куран воие аӈкильы, па льын эльтайн иса пальман вантль. Акайн па машья нях вешн войль льапатльальы. Пальман, хурыман ульты войль льапатмаль юпиян, апщеӈальаль ястас:

– Там унт вой. Ханты хоятн кураӈ воя аяльа. Посальн уятсэм, кармас кутн, юх льэра тахарьамаль, курль шукатмаль. Аӈкельн манэм маса, льув па посаль папелка ущман манс. Муӈ ин ай нёпиев тумтакльальэв, щаха сусн вельщи унта аӈкель хоща китльэв. Ин нын льувель льаптальн, па шавияльан. Льув хольна ай, хоят эльты пальаль. Хоты, кашащльатан?

Хильыеӈальаль муя ант кашащльатан. Сэмльан аль ропсальльатан. Нюр войн хоща катальты вуратльатан. Вельщи шияльам от хоты.

– Ма, ма, манэм мии мисьйиӈк кеван! – хащ кутармаман кеванан хоща вуратты питсатан.

– Рома ульатан! Кутарматы питльатан, унаӈкана ястальам, льув льапатльальы. Там хатль, ольанан Соръёхан апщием нёпие ат льапаталь. Наӈ па етна пелья воиен льапатльэн, ма наӈен нётльэм, – нох, ёша альэмаса, акаяльн Питльор эвие.

– Ям щи, етн ки етн ат уль, – Питльор эвие кашащас. Уртыель ивевн ольӈашак мольты верн миййльыльа, льув па иса щалитман тайльа, куш кепа льув такан льаӈхалья муй вер, иса ольӈа верты. Акаяльн тахты туты парса. Унаӈкельн тахтыйн льэпаӈ льыпи эльты маса. Ин нёпиель тахты эльты потсэль, потам мув эльты ант ат потльа. Мет кашаӈа щаха йиты верыталь.

Тови хатльат ёхи хащсат, ущ ёхатты тыльащ ольаӈ наяӈ хатльат ёхатсат. Щи онтасан Най ими хув хошам. каврам ёшльальн нёпие аяльтыена щи вощхиты питсальы. Няврэмӈан ищи най хошмальтам мува иль опсамтыльтан, войн вощхиман. Хут талья йис, льын там хульаӈ Ас, льантаӈ Ас посаль мувн хухатльытан вуш эльты. Там воие па вельщи сэма питс, щи онтасан щалитсаљљан. Хоят вантмаљ антом, вой вантмаљ антом, туп аҧкељ уйтас. Там няпрэмҧан вељщи љув сэмаља питсатан. Щишн куш кепа паљман, хурыман ищипа љын хощайн аяљтыена таља-сас, мосаҧ ищи ям хоятҧан. Ант кетамљаљљан, ант сэҧкљаљљан.

Намн, Ас йиҧкаљ па тэрмаљаман йиҧкљаљ щарс пеља туљљы, мохет па ий лотн тата уљты хащљат, ущ хуљ љаваљман. Там љув сэма питам мувељ, энмам лотэљ. Наяҧ хатљат онтасан ешавуљ лыптат, тор-нат, ванши мув эљты энамаљ. Хошма йиљ. Емаҧ ханты мувељ ищи хош-маљтыяљ, хорам, арсыр лыпат эљты хорамаҧа йиљ.

Љапаткем туп хащас, хув кураҧ воие љув курљаљн хухатљыты питас. Соръёхан похие, Питљор эвие пиљн нёпиян каман щира ол-мащиман, мисьйиҧк кеван љув эљтайљ нох нирэмаљљан, щаљта иљ ханятыљтан торн кутн. Воянан, ванта, ат кашљайтан. Щиты ханятыман ёнтљатан, љынан каш, войн па ликащаљ. Уятташ юпиян, ох пушхаљн щаљта вотэмаљайтан па, ељ раканљатан. Хой хољљаљ, хой няхаљ.

– Минэман нюхаљљэн ки, мисьйиҧкан маљэман, ат уятљэн ки, љэљљы хащљан!

Щимащ пощтуљ нявтэмҧан нёпие љухасҧаљаљ устан. Нёпиян еша нохман, љын юпанан хатљ хуват щи хухатљыяс. Ешавуљ войн юраҧа йис, нохты муйн вољыяс, курљ тумтакљас. Тумтака ювмаљ юпиян, та-кан хухатљыты питс. Няврэмҧан сора эљты ёхатљаљљы. Хатљ хуват, ванши этмаљ юпиян, унаҧканан ванши сухатты парљайтан. Нёпие няр ваншийн юран тываљља уҧаљ вусаља, љув па љухаљты ант љаҧхаља, ељ хухаљаљ. Љувељ туп мисьйиҧк мосаљ.

– Муй иса нёљасљан, муй хорпи охсар хорпи вой! Љэва ванши, щаха аты энамљан.

Тумељ љын пељаян тыш ант тайљ. Туп кущайљ ёхатаљ хољапљаљ эљты, нёпайљ мохты наварман ныкљы кутартљаљљы. Юхур хопљ вана љаваљман, йиҧка руҧкамтаљ. Щи кут ай кущайҧаљаљ эљты вољљы ёрэмаљљы. Ун кущаяљн апаљмиља, вощхиља, љапатља. Куш намаљта ёхатаљ, хоп љыпия ахун саккар ханятаљ па, саккаран лукемаља. Ин воие, ай няврэмат иты саккар љухаљман ешащаљ. Иљампа аҧкељан щиты ант шависа љуљн, хоты Юхурн щалитса. Хун Юхур хољапљаљ вантман хув кеша янхас, нёпие Питљор эвие аҧкељн љапатља. Ай Соръёхан нэ хот тэљ вой љапатаљ. Ай нёпие ищи љув щи мисьйиӈкан ищаљтаљљы. Љуӈан, наян, пељӈаян хатљат порайн, н响врэмат унаӈки тонты хот лаӈкас. Атаљн ољљыты ёлах ураӈан. Хатљаљн муйн пељӈайт шек тонты хот љыпия ант љонљат, пусӈи пут хатљ хуват ов пуӈаљан омасаљ. Юхур ищи хашапаљ тонты хот љыпиян ярсаљљы. Етн, туп ољты љэщатыты иљ питљ, кураӈ воиељ тата тащ љояљ. Хот љыпия љонаљ, љављасаљ. Хун кущайљ хашап љыпия љонаљ. Юхур ищи матты войљ пеља вер ант тайљ, љув пељайљ аты ватљ, хашап љыпия љоӈаљ. Щаљта, хотаӈ тохаљљаљн пељӈайљаљ ким ёваљтаљ юпиян, хашап ий пелак сайљ нох аљэмаљљы. Тум пелак хашап эљты Питљор эвие уртыељ пиљн хашап љыпи эљты кимљы аӈкармиман љављасман, омасљатан. Љављасљатан, хун нёпиян шанша омасман, акайн хашап љыпия ваӈкаљ. Хашап љыпиян, љув нявромат иты, кущайљ курљаљ пуӈаљан иљ љэщатыяљ, па ешавуљ норхиман иљ щи вояпља. Юхур, анкељн щи куш лявтыљыља, муя љув унт вой щиты атма утаљљаљљы. Па ванта, љувеља ищи щаль нёпиељ, юхат аӈкељ вољыяс щит эљты потартты. Хув кураӈ воиељ утљас па, кашаӈ етн хашап љыпия вуратас. Пељӈа эљты шек паљман ус, щи ураӈан кущаяљн утаљтаса шаш вурн хашап љыпия ваӈкты. Курљаљ ванта хуват, шушман хашап љыпия љонтыйс ки, хашапаљ љуљн таљаӈ тэљн маншисљы. Няврэмӈан ищиты такан љаӈхасайтан акайн хашап љыпийн ољљыты, туп ун аӈканан тохи хун эсаљљайтан.

– Аљаӈсахат акайн рупитты манљ, щи арат хољп вантты мосљ, љашкуп унты яӈхты, хуљ туты. Хатљ кат пуш хољапљаљ вантљаљљы, яљап хуљљаљ ант ат няхисат. Халывљаљ муйн таљаӈ хатљ нељљат, љувиљаљ тохи эсаљљайт ки, ий хуљ ат хащаљ.

Няврэмӈан хољна хув хашап љыпи эљты кимљы вантман омасљатан. Љављасман, хун Най иман иљ ољты манљ. Ешавуљ љын хољна вояпљайтан, Най иман еша щутщаты Ас папелакан опсамтыяљ, па ељљы шушмаљ. Љуӈ хуват ољты кумљ антом. Нови атаӈ хатљ, љуӈ сыс љув иса Турам хуват шушиљыяљ, щутщаты кум ант шитаљ.

Хатљаљн Питљор эвие па Сорљёхан похие Харыпаты пеља мисљан канщты ивевн китыљыљайтан. Юхљы мувн, щита мисат пељӈайт эљты шаващљат. Кураӈ войн ищи љын юпанан мисат канщты хухатљыяљ, утща ёльан омасты век кеша ант кашащас. Ай кущайŋальаль эльты ивевн нянь вохман, амп иты, льын юпанан хухатлыяс. Кущайŋальаль торн кутн куш ханятыман хонтатльыльтан, ищипа льынан уятльальлы. Ох пушхальн такан поткальлы, ищи матты асталь:

– Миятан нянь!

Куш кепа каши, па хоты верты, мисат па мосль ёхи канышты. Етна пелья мисат ёхи нюхальтан юпиян, Питльор эвие аŋкель мис пусты камн омасаль, нёпия ищи тата ваныен льавльасман льоялы. Туп мис пусты Ай Соръёхан нэ питщаль, мохты ох пушахан поткалья:

– Ма эльтэм аль ёрэми, ма тата наŋ пуŋльэнан льойльам!

Еша мис путль кутпаль унты ёхаталь, Питльор эвие аŋкель ветрайль эльты мисьйиŋкаль атэльт пута шошемальлы, кураŋ воялья. Тумель тащ мисьйиŋк инщемаль, няврэмат унаŋки хоща хонталь. Щильта па нянь вохаль. Няврэмат унаŋки ивевн ханты ернас щеп льыпийн нянь сопасман патн тутльыяс. Юхур аŋкийн воие ищи щалитман вощхилья, нянян льапатлья, потартыман:

– Нянь пулэн льэви! Шек ар нянь наŋена ант рахаль льэты, нынана ай отата туп эплльаŋ льэтот мосаль, саккараŋ льэтот. Наŋ льухасŋальан ищиты туп мампащ вохльатан. Щит хоты нын мет мосты льэтотан. Наŋен хоты мав вольлы ант рахаль, хонэн кашия йиль, нянь льухлья па, пильŋальан хоща, ёнттыя хухальма. Щи, щи тармаль, па ант тайльам!

Нёпие щи ощхуля няньль пулэмальлы. Йи пелкаль иль луттальлы. Хув куральн нянь пулаль ванашак хатальтальлы, ищи матты, хойтыйн нох нярэмалья. Ий пулаль льухальталь юпиян, кимет пулаль па нёльэмальлы. Ямас льэталь юпиян камн альльыты кур пуŋальан иль керытлыяль, пусаŋ пут пуŋальан, пельŋайн ант ат порлья. Няврэмат унаŋки па курль пуŋальан хатль хуват шумах верман омасаль.

– Аль кетмальн кураŋ войн, – няврэмат пелья унаŋкан ивевн ястыяль, шумах вой пальман. – Нын войн, нын тумпиян, эльты шавиман тайлья льуŋхатн. Льув ищи ун куща тайль. Нын льувель кетамльальн ки, нынана атам.

– Хойн льув шавилья? – няврэмат инщмасат.

– Льув хоты Тураман мальы шавилья, льуŋхатн эльты тайлья. Муŋ ханты мирэв, кашаŋ хоят льув льуŋх тайль. Щи онтасан емаŋ войт ант рахаль кетамты. Мет ай нипсар имен холъна пуратты ант рахалъ. Туняль, аль па нумльалъльан, хоты мисыкут ими кев шукан лап ёвальсальн?

– Унанки, мин щиты па нулама ант ульаман! – щи вер нумальмаман, нябрэмӈан ястастан, – мин нумассаман, нёпиемн лыльаӈ мисыкут ими льухльапльальы.

Ёнтман, нулама наварнэ вусльан па, нампаран, кевшукан лап ёвальсальан. Кураӈ войн хоты ёнтты туп льаӈхаса, щимащ вой ёхи хун льавемальльы. Вельсальльан, амуй туман хонтас, хой вантас. Мисыкут ими ищипа шукатсальльан.

Ищи хатальан, етн, Питльор эвие аӈкель тураль амуйн лап туса, кашия йис. Лыпель вольльы лап матса. Льальты кемль антом ус. Унаӈкан, пощтуль нябрэмат эльты инщмас:

– Наварнэ ант вантсатан, кетамман антом? Йиӈк Урр Ими муй ураӈан ликащас, муя эвиель лыльаль лап сухтаслы, льальты щираль вольльы антом. – Хой муй накльат верас? Аӈкель ураӈан такан пальтамаман, Питльор эвие иса потартсальльы, хоты лын мисыкут ими нампаран лап ёвальсальльан. Ун ими, Юхур похль, наварнэ ими посн шошамты партсальльы. Йиӈк Урр Ими пелъа пойкащты мосаль. Акайн посль верталь эльты унаӈкан Турам ащель пелъа пойкащман эвиель пуӈальан опсас. Йиӈкан муйн мийльыльльы, мевльаль эльты хошам ёшальн эльты катльыман, хутльаталь унты щи опсас. Похальн, наварнэ посль верам юпиян, щитль хорамаӈ охшама, посль ёвармаслы, льуӈхльалъа хот льоӈльа понты партсальльы. Похаль охшама ёвармам посль нох льуӈхльалъа си туслы. Ун ими па пасан верас, порыльыты, инщтот опсамтыяс. Юхат хольыена шай инщты омассат. Ин тальта ельльы мисыкут ими посальн льув хоталь, льув руталь шавилъа. Нулама ульам нябрэмӈан ищи тата ванан омассатан, льавльасман, хун лын накльатан туӈа щира льэщатльа. Хильэӈальаль ольты китмаль юпиян, ун ими хольна хув опсас эвель пуӈальан. Альаӈсахат, нох верьаман кемн, нябрэмӈан Питльор эвие аӈкель шияльастан. Льув нох кильмаль, хольна кашаӈ хорпи, туп шушильыман, мисльаль пусты манс. Ин тальта ельльы, нябрэмӈан туп наварнэ шияльальтан, ель хухальман манльатан, еман вой муй нуран кетамты.

– Ма хун айие усам, – унаӈкан потартыяль, – катра ивевн якты хот верльа. Мохет якты актыщильат. Порыльыльат, ёнтльат, емаӈ арат арыљат, апщиев пеља пойкащљат. Нумтэмн, кураŋ вой ураŋан ищи якты хот верља. Кураŋ вой ищи емаŋ. Нёхељ љэты рахаљ, туп пойкащты ищи мосаљ. Нёхиљы, хуљљы ханты хоят хун па верытаљ уљты, – щит ханты хоят уљапса. Щаха сусн патлама йитаљ кемн, нын Турам пеља аŋкармиятн, љув хорљ нумн љойљ. Там войн Турамн такан щалитља. Ма нынан љув монщаљ ин монщљэм. Ипуш, катра, йис порайн, – унаŋкан па щи монщты питс, – хуљам ху вой вељман, кураŋ вой нюхаљман хухаљсат. Ин эљты ёхатљэљ, там ёхатљэљ. Воељ вољљы метмаљ, аплак хуват щи куш навармияљ, щёмљы питам вой эљты щи ин ёхатља. Турам ащев, нумн љапат хоптыйн хољта пеља таŋха манты верљ ус. Иљљы аŋкармас, метам войљ шияљасљы, щаля версаљљы. Щаљ вераљн кураŋ войљ Турма нох сухтасљы. Ин щиŋанща хуйŋан таљты хащсатан.

– Унаŋки! Муя па тухаљ войт ем тайљат, муя љувиљаљ кетамты ант рахаљ?

– Љув малы ханты хоят шавиљат. Щит муŋ љуŋхљув. Нынан ищи шавиљат. Нын љуŋхљан пеља атам верљатан ки, хойн па нын щаха нётљайтан. Хоят ий пища хун хойљыяљ, ий вера хун питыљыяљ.

Ун ими щи кутн хуљљаљ љэщатты кум шитаљ, па хиљыљаља каман потар вераљ. Щи онтасан љын рома омасљатан. Љуŋ кутопан хуљ сора шакаљ, щишн ун ими яљап хуљљаљ эљты шумах вераљ. Няхиям отљаљ эљты вой вущмаљтаљ. Ёшљаљ иса сора, каркама рупитљат.

– Ма Кати Най имийн шавиљайм, Касам найн. Наŋ, похие, Љэв Кутап икийн шавиљайн, Сорни Турам кутап похаљн.

– Мун Кураŋ воев Турам хуват уљты хоятат ищи шавийљ?

– Љув ищи шавиты хоят тайљ, хота љув уљљат, ма ант уятљэм. Љув емаŋ вой хоты, ищи рут тайљ. Наŋ па, эвие, љуŋх тайљан!

– Ма уятљэм, ма Ханшаŋ Орыйн, Эляŋ Орыйн шавиљайм, наŋ манэм ар пуш потартысан. Щи ураŋан, ма ампат ант кетамљаљљам.

– Яна щи, наŋ ащен, наŋ рутљан, иса хољыена Эляŋ Орыйн, Ханшаŋ Орыйн шавиљайт. Апљан щи онтасан такан шавияљан. Яма љаптаљн.

– Ма ивевн апљам љапатљаљљам, ант кетамљаљљам.

Унаŋкан хуљ верты соŋхљаљ шанш эљты пуŋља потсаљљы. Курљаљ еша моратман, вощхисљы:

– Хей-я! Таљаŋ љапат Паљŋат љойљат. Ин Икиљан век кеша таŋха љойты питљат. Еша марэмаљат, па вољыљат. Ерта аты йиљ. Курыиљљам щи љоват войн порљайт. Ертсат ки, курљам љуљн войн порты вољытсайт.

– Унаŋки, муй Икет тата љойљат? Куртэвн ий Ики антом.

– Марэматы, Паљŋан Икиљам эљты потартыљам. Ерта йис ки, паљаŋљаљ љуљн матсат.

– А-аа! – нохљы, Турам пеља аŋкармиман, эвие нюхмас, – щи мољты Икиљан!

Щи марэматы Икиљаљ эљты нуврэмŋан такан паљсатан. Хун Љэв Кутап ики љовљаљ хомщийн рэскаљљы, Турам патлама ювантыяљ. Щаљта марыты питљ па, сам щах ахољта пеља манљ, ищи матты кевт лакки лосытты вуратљат.

– Охшамљан ямашак яраљан, ант рахаљ няр охты марыты кемн хухатљыты. Антом ки щаха охљан, ай порайн вотљайт. Пиращ имеŋан, икеŋан иты, нови, вотам охсохан шушиљыты питљатан. Нын айŋан,– унаŋкан па ястас, – хухатљытан эљты щёŋхры хуŋхран эљты ерт вохатан. Ертаŋа похалљаљ манљат ки, курљам кена йиљат.

– Яна, ма нумљэм, туняљ, щёŋхры хуŋхры эљты ерт вохсам!
Щёŋхры, хуŋхры акем ики
Вурэм шепам вет сот
Вурэм шепам хут сот
Акем ики эљты
Ертаŋ паљаŋ воха.

– Унаŋки! Наŋ курљан хота кашитљат? – ёшииљљаљ унаŋкељ шанша понман, ищи матты хуљантыман, маты лотн унаŋкељ курљаљ войн порљайт, инщасас Питљор эвие. – Ма мољхатљ иљ ракантсам, курэм шек каши ус, еша омассам, курэм вољыяс кашитты. Ин иса ям. Наŋ ищи еша рома опса.

– Нын ай курљан муя кашитљат, нынан сора хухатљыты мосљ. Наŋ курыиљљан нэмољты порайн ант ат кашитљат. Ант ат љуљн уятљан, хоты љув войн порљайт… Щи омасљув, ята! Хуљыиљљув па ољљат.

Похие! Эвие! Яŋхатан са имайн ими хоща! Каматса хуљн туваљн, нярхуљ ат љэљ.

Вељщи љэты етшам няврэмŋан вешљан мормаŋа йистан. Ватушка имайн ими хоща, хуљ тутљытанан порайн мампащ пиљн шайн ищаљтыљайтан. Ин па љын щикем эплљаŋа, яма љэстан, ий мампащ хон љыпия ант љэпаљ. Амуй номасан унаŋканан љэты юпиян тохи китыљыљайтан. Љэвман ељпи тохи хухатљыстан ки, муй арат мав, печеник каш ураŋан хон љыпия љуљн манамтас. Я, хоты верты, хуљљан аљэмаман, имайн ими хоща хухаљман матсатан.

– Љоятан са, љыям мисьйиŋк ёрэмасам понтыя, љув нянь пиљн шек харщи там љэтот хоща.

Хиљэŋаљљаљ ищи матты хољта пеља тапсатан, хув тахайн, наман хухаљтан щащаљ.

– Щахашак ма ки шушиљыљам, хуљљам љэщаттэм юпиян, муйљ йи лотн омасты, – аяљта нох вортасман омасты лотаљ эљты, унаŋкан љув сахатаљ ястас.

Соръёхан похие осхиељ пиљн щи љоват сора хухаљман матсатан па, Питљор эвие щёŋхры хуŋхры шияљас, туп уваљты вутщияс, ерт вохман, торн кута тахрамтас, иљ ракнас, хуљаљ ищи ељ, ванши кута ракнас. Лыпат эљты щёŋхры хуŋхры эвие ещаљт, иљ љатамтас.

– Щёŋхры хуŋхры акем ики! Наŋ марыты Ун Икиљан эљты ерт воха! – шитаман ястас Питљор эвие, – унаŋкем курљаљ войн порљайт, шек кашитљат, туп шушиљыљат. Ерт мантаљ юпиян, курљаљ тумтака йиљат. Ун Икиљан унты пурљыя, муя ертэљ нямартљэљ, яма ат ертаљ.

Щёŋхры хуŋхры ищи матты ай эвие ясŋат хуљмас, хорам лыптаљ эљты нох пурљас, амуй хољта пеља арыман манмаљ ныља. Питљор эвие хуљаљ нох аљэмас, ищи ељљы хухаљмас, уртыељ эљты нюхаљман.

Ватушка иман няврэмат хуљ тувман туп шияљас, пасаныељ нык аљэмасљы. Шай путљ валэмасљы. Пасанаља каман мампащ, параник понамтас. Ай отŋан, шай туп аљ понамтыљтан лопсах ана. Еша инщемаљтан, мампащ порэмаљтан. Параник кемн юр антом, вељщи љэвам хонљана антшак љэпаљ. Мампащ анан пеља аŋкармиљтан. Хољыена анан хољљат, щаха унаŋкан ељэма верљаљљан. Хоят хоща мавŋ љэтот ант рахаљ патэљ унты таљтапты. Ешавуљ, пуŋљa пасан эљты хатапсатан. Ватушка анљаљ нох мухсаљљы. Пасан љаращ љыпия потсаљљы, пасанљ вутышак нёхтаслы. Ин хоты рахаљ ёхи хухаљты. Муй арат айкељ ус, хољыена ун имия потарсаљљан. Муй хуват хољна хоят хотн мойљантыты. Ёхи тэрматсатан. Ватушка иман ими ищи хуљљаљ љэщатты љоямтас.

Етна пеља турам вољљы патлас, мараŋ отљаљ такан сыяљсат. Ин Икен љовљаљ таŋха такан хомщийн рэскаслы. Унаŋкан, тонты хотљ овљ лап петсаљљы, няврэмŋан охшамљан ох пата сухтаслы, ёш эљты нярэмаман, ёхи, паварт хотаља шушмас.

– Ун Икиљан љовљаљ щи навармасат, ин ерта йиљ. Иљампа щёŋхры хуŋхры акан икийн хуљсайтан, ястасат Паљнаŋ Икиљана. Щи сыяљсат. Туп кум шитсат ёхи љоŋемиты, ертаљ аљ щёшантас.

Сус пора каш хатљат

Љуŋ хатљат ёхи хащсат, сус пеља Турмаљ хатэмас. Унаŋкан аљŋа таŋха нох киљас. Љопасаљ эљты ёраŋ хирљаљ ким аљэмамаљ. Ахой ураŋан мойљантыты пормас каштаљ ныља. Уртые, осхиељ пиљн мохты ищмастан, хољта пеља унаŋкан љэщатыяљ.

– Там хатљ мояŋ хоятн ёхатљаюв.

Мољхатљ, љын ёнттан эљты, ахун рущ ими ёхтыљымаљ тум, сойм папелак курт пелка, няврэмат интерната акаттаљ. Ин щишн яйљан, опиљан, ныйљан хољыена тохи Яљап воша утаљтыты манты верэљ уљ. Там хатљ унаŋкељ похљаљ, меньљаљ, няврэмат пиљн хољыена, там соям пелка, ун љапкая йиљат. Щи ураŋан унаŋкан мойљантыты верљ уљ. Матты меняља таŋха, ун охшам, хирљ эљты нох сухтас. Кутап похаљ хорамаŋ вайн там тови ёнтсаљљы. Щи ељпи хатљ, ун тутаŋ хоп ёхтыљыяс, турам сот пормас ампара аљљыса. Камн кеванаŋ, хошапаŋ љаращ туса. Љэтотаŋ љаращат, щашканы хиртэљт. Маваŋ хошапат, вои путат. Ай отŋан хатљ хуват пормас аљљыты ёх пеља вантман, пушасн хоща тахрапмас, тяттистан. Хатљ хуват щи аљљысат ёх, меттэљ унты.

Ешавуљ яна щи соям папелак эљты акайљаљ ёхатсат. Хотэљн ар нясврэм эљты сый па каш. Сорљёхан похие Питљор эвие пиљн аматсатан, щи арат хоят ёхатмељ эљты. Утща ёнтты иса кашљы марэмасайтан. Мохет пиљн, Питљор эвие уртыељ пиљн ищи љапкая шушмастан. Хув кураŋ нёпиян ищи љапкая мохет юпиян шушмас.

– Нёпиев ищи пормас ԓутты ԓаӈхаԓа, – ун отат няхман ястасат.

– Аӈки! – амтатԓыман Питԓор эвие хоятат кутн наварман, анкеԓ хоща апаԓмас, – мин ищи вурты нуй ԓутԓаман, нёпиема сапаԓ сох ёнтԓам, авкаем иты. Ёнтасты ма питԓам.

– Ԓутԓаман, ԓутԓаман! – аӈкеԓ нюхмас, – муй арат пормас туса, муй наӈен мосаԓ, иса ԓутԓаман. Анта вурты нуй, наӈен восты нуй ԓутԓаман.

– Ма наӈен сакан вуԓэм, – унаӈкеԓ ястас, – аӈкен сакԓаԓ хоԓыена ԓыԓатсаԓԓан. Хиԓы ёшиеԓ пирщ, каркам ёшаԓан ищи матты кентан апаԓмасԓы.

– Наӈ щаха ма пиԓэмн омасԓан па, нёпиен хорамаӈ сапаԓ сохн ёнтԓэн. Ханшийн муйн мин ԓув сапаԓ сохԓ хорамԓаԓэмн. Питԓор эвие, амтатԓыман унаӈкеԓ хошам, пирщемам, мормаӈ ёш апаԓмасԓы. Щи арат хоят яха ёхтас хоты, няврэм ԓыпи аԓ арыяс, аԓ якас. Каш, умащ хорпи хатԓ. Еша унаӈкеԓ пуӈаԓан хухатԓыяс, щиӈанща нёпиеԓ пиԓн апаԓтантыты питс, валэмиман ёш сурн, муй арат мосмаԓ сапаԓ сохаԓа, восты нуй. Уртыеԓ ищи такан амтас, аӈкеԓ ёхтам верн.

– Ма наӈен мет хорамаӈ ханшийн сапаԓ сохен ёнтԓэм. Восты нуйԓ хоща хорамаӈ хойм ԓыпат хорпи ханшийн унаӈкем партԓэм эватты. Кашаӈ хоят умащԓыты питԓ, – нёпиеԓ апаԓмаман Питԓор эвие ястас.

Ԓапкайн, кашан хоят каман хорпи турам сот пормас ԓутас. Питԓор эвие кутап акаяԓн, па ай акаяԓн ищи, кат ермак ернас сохн ԓутса. Унаӈкеԓ яна сак ԓутас. Аӈкеԓ яԓап кат хорпи нуйн маншиса, ун пук эԓты. Хув курпи воиеԓа воԓԓы тармаԓ. Питԓор эвие пуӈаԓн ԓойман, аӈкеԓ пуӈԓа хатамас.

– Аӈки! Манэм товар ԓута!

Амуй товар эвеԓ вохаԓ хоты, вантмаԓ? Ай Соръёхан нэ хоԓна маваӈ ԓэтот вохас ԓапка нэӈаԓ эԓты. Каԓы сак шияԓамаԓ кемн, эвеԓа сак ԓутас.

– Ант ԓаӈхаԓаям мампащ! – мохет пеԓа еԓэм вантты ураӈан, Питԓор эвие ниӈхарԓаты питс, – Товар ԓута!

Рущ ясаӈ ант уятман, пормасаԓ ант хошсаԓԓы ястаты. Ԓапкая ёхтам мохет сыяӈа потрэматы питсат, амуй мосаԓ Питԓор эвия. Еԓэма верам кемн, эвие аӈкелъ вутаӈ нуй сах пон лъыпия ханемас. Щита иса машьяя йис. Хув кураӈ воиелъ ищи нулама ох пушхалъ ахой молъты хир лъыпия лукемамалъ, хоятат Питлъор эвие пилън потартантытэлъ элъты. Ин щалъта нёпие мощатса, лъапка элъты ким лукемаса. Лъапка нэӈалъ, норм хошапалъ пелки пушмасъы, Питлъор эвие тохи вохсалълъы.

– Юва! Ты юва ям эвие! Али, муй наӈен мосалъ, муя талътахийн ниӈхарлъалъан, аӈкенан муй мосалъ, иса щи лъутсайн!

Лъапкая ёхтам мохет иса машьяя йисат, амуй товар эвилэӈки вохалъ. Лъапка хот лъыпийн иса шитама йис. Питлъор эвие палъман хурыман аялъташак лъапка норм лъыпия аӈкелъ пона катлъасман шушмас. Аӈкелъ рома йи лотн хащас лъойты. Щишн эвие поналъ сорая эслъапсалълъы па лъыпия лъоӈемас. Ун норм хуват, нумалъта арсыр нёхеӈ колбаса лъэтотат тахартамат, щит вохман ешалъас. Ёшалън тохи катлъамтыяс сорая, па ар мирн няха алъмам юпиян, ялъпа аӈкелъ нуй сах пон илъпия ханемас.

– Щимащ молъты товар улъмалъ! – такан лъапка тэлъыя акмам хоят, няхман ешащсат, – муӈ па нумаслъув, лъувелъ эплъаӈ лъэтот мосалъ.

Товарн лъутам юпиян, нявврэм елъэмалъан ким хухалъмас. Соръёхан похие лъапка лъыпиян хащас. Лъувелъ таӈха ищи молъты товар мосас. Ин щиӈанща рущ лъэтоталъ пилън, эви, хув кураӈ воиелъ пилън ёхи шушмастан. Шуштан элъты, катӈан колбаса шупан ёхи лъухалъсалълъан. Нёпие, вер ант уятман, нёхеӈ лъэтот ёхи авашсалълъы. Хотан унты ёхатманан, лъэтотан холъас. Кур пуӈалъан омасты ветрайт элъты ямас няр йиӈк инщсатан. Еша улъман хонлъан щи мощатсайт. Питлъор эвие хоныелъ щи лъоват моратты питса, няр ванши элъты илъ олъас. Кутн нох лъоямтыман, па няр йиӈк инщемияс. Хонлъ кашия йис, щалъта охтысыты питщас. Нёпиелъ ищи ветрайлъ элъты пуӈлъа манты кемлъ антом ус, катлъэм ветра няр йиӈк инщас. Потам мув элъты керытлъыман, щита аӈкелъ ёхатмалън, Питлъор эвие, нёпиелъ пилън уятсалълъы. Колбаса лъэтотан холъыена илъ охатман. Нёпие, курлъалъ лакки ёвалъман, ищиты керытлъыяс. Аӈкелъ сорая леккар вохты вош, вуты пелъа хухалъман манс. Юхат, эвелъ тумтака ювмалъ юпиян ясталъ, щимащ рущ лъэтот нэмолъты порайн па аты вулъ. Нявврэмат хащ ат халъсат ат рахты товар элъты. Етна пелъа ай отӈан тумтака йистан, туп рущ лъэтот элъты ин аты лъаӈхасайтан хулъты.

Сусн Питлъор эвие, ныйлъалъ, уртылъалъ уталътыты тусайт. Ин лъонщ питтаљ унты няврэм љын хощайн па ант ёхатаљ. Щаха, таљн щутщаты ёхаттэљ порайн туп айкељ туљат, хоты школайн утаљтыљат.

Щи сус нохар юхт хољыена нохаран энапсайт. Юхур, нохар пошмаљ пора кемн, унта љэщатыты питс. Вояљ, вуљыљаљ нётайљы хащсат муйн. Нётты хоят таяљ. Унта яŋхты, хиљэŋаљљаљ шек харщеŋан.

– Аљаŋсахат, амуй унта манљатан? Хаљыват унта яŋхљув. Нохар сэŋкљув, нёта акатљув. Воев нётайљы хащас, таљ нянян уљ. Вуљыљув, Эраптайн, ищи нётаељ хољас. Муŋ хоты кашаŋ хатљ љэљув, инщљув. Войљув ищи љэты љаŋхаљайт, – акайян љынана потартыяљ, – хуљ, нёхи љэты љувиљаља ант рахаљ. Нётаељ – щит љув мосты љэтотэљ.

– Хув кураŋ воев ищи муŋ пиљэвн хопн янхаљ?

– Анта, љув пан хуват муŋ юпеват хухаљаљ. Муŋ Эрапта унты яŋхљув, ваныена. Вуљыљув муйн вантљаљљув.

– Ма, мет ољна актащљам! Ма! Ма! – кутљанан хащ ант кутармаман, ин отŋан актащты питсатан.

Унаŋкан эљты сопек вохты хухаљмастан. Унаŋкан хуван ванан сопек љэщатмаљ, љэтоты хирн муйн понмаљ. Иса тащ, ахун иса мощтаљљы, муй мосаљ. Иса кум шитаљ, нэмољты ант ёрэмаљ. Каматса таљ хир понмаљ, нохар па нёта понты ураŋан. Няврэмŋан нюки вайљан сора, тэрмаљаман нох эхсаљљан, курљана сопекљан хошкаман. Ин там порайн хун па верытља нюки вайн яŋхты, панаљ вощлахаŋ. Сойм хувн сорс. Хопт муйн, посаљ пелак љойљат, туп ёвра пуратљан, мохты вощлаха рукљан. Сора актащман, патан љэтоты хир, таљ хирт аљэмаман, няврэмŋан хухаљман акайн юпийн матсатан. Нёпайн љын юпанан навармас. Хув курљаљн хухаљман, љув хољнаољŋашак нык ёхтас. Рэп иљпийн кущайљ пуŋљашак рахаљтыяс па, аљ шушамтыяљ. Юхур нык ёхатмаљн, войљ пуŋља нюхаљсаљљы. Хоп љыпия ант эсљыљљы. Няврэмŋан па, хаш юх нувт вощлаха ёвљам лотн эљты, рома хопа љэљсатан. Акайн пеља такан хуљатман уљљатан, ант нянярљыљтан, антом ки, хопљ эљты хољна ељ парљайтан. Сора мотораŋ хопн яŋхты хољна ат ликамтыяљ, љын ищи шек вуйљыљайтан патн. Љуŋн йи пуш хопа љэљљысайтан. Шек ям. Ин ищи, акайн мотораљ сухтасљы, хопљ нёхљас. Орыман, посљ хуват мотораŋ хопн Эраптаељ унты, вот иты манты питс, ищи матты нох пурљаты вуратаљ.

Кураŋ воељ хоп љыпия куш такан вуратас. Кущайљаљ хоп туп нохљы нёхљас, љув намн каман щира якты питс, ат моштаман, хољта пеља хухаљты. Йиŋка рукты паљљыяс, йиŋкан аљ морља. Щаљта таŋха нумаљмасљы, љуŋ хуват кущайљ юпиян пан хуват хухатљыяс, ин ищи наварман, хоп юпиян нёхтасљы. Хопељ эљты, ёхи аты хащљ, юраŋ мотор юпиян ий кемн хухаљаљ. Хой ишн хољна ољŋа питамтыяљ, щаљта кущайљаљ љаваљман љойљ. Унта, нётайŋ лотэљ хоща ёхатмељ кемн, вуты хойты кемељн, нёпиељ йиŋка, хопељ пеља навармас. Љув таŋха нумасаљ, кущайљам ма урŋемн вуты хойты верэљ уљ. Ин щиŋанща воиељ вощлаха иљ вуншантас, иљ љонас. Љувељан варс хун ныља. Щи куш тащ варс пан хуват понман ус. Хопаŋ мохет љэр тахайн вуты хойљыљат. Нёпиељ па ульня лота навармас. Хув, ващ курыиљљаљ мохты щи вощлаха хувљасат. Љув љуљн паљтамаман вуты навармаљ. Отшам вой хоты, мет ныкљы, хоп хоща вуратаљ. Щитаљн хонљ вуша, вољљы иљ руŋкас. Иљ шуйљамаљ кемн, таљ охиељн ељ ёхи кератман љойљ. Кущайљ пеља щаль сэмн вантыман. Юхур, хопљ эљты вуты навармас. Варс морытман. Юш верты питс, воиељ хоща. Апщенаљаљ пеља уваљтас:

– Торн сухтатан. Муŋ ин воев вощлах эљты нох сухтаљэв!

Питљор эвие, уртыељ пиљн вољљы паљтамастан, воиян ураŋан. Нык этман кемн, мохты торн сухаттты питщастан. Торн щир па антом, таљ песљаŋ. Ёшљан вура пељсайт. Питљор эвие щи куш каркама па сора песљаŋљ маншияс, ешавуљ хащ хољљапа ант питс, щи љоват вурн этсайт. Картэŋ сэвљаљ муйн ивевн веш пеља раканљат, торастаман. Щи куш шаш пеља ювтылљылљы, туп иљ ниншапаљ, љув торасэљн па иљљы ёвљасљат. Соръёхан похие нык, хопаљ пеља хухаљман манс. Осхиељ нумасаљ, иљампа уртыем метс, щи манс. Љув па хољљаман ељљы песљаŋаљ сухатты питщас. Нёпиељ вощлаха иљ аљ шуйљаљ, хольща щимащ вой љув па хољна мощатљат. Воиељ апщи юкана йис. Љув такљэљ уљты пищ антом, щиты љув хощайљ утаљсат.

– Та, кеши вуя! – Соръёхан похие вуты ёхатмаљ, кеши осхеља ниншамтас, – кешийн песљаŋен эвты.

– Яна щи! – Питљор эви амтас. Унаŋкељ ивевн песљаŋ кешийн эватмийљ.

Ин щиӈанща муй арат торн, муй песъаӈ эватсатан, хољыена акаяна аљтысљан, вана йиӈк пуӈља тусљан. Љув ищи ям арат торн маншимаљ, па варс моратмаљ. Торанљаљ ващ кеља, сэв иты сэвсаљљы. Няврэмӈан акайн пеља вантман, нумассатан, амуй љув верты вутщияљ?

– Кељэв куља йиљ ки, воев понямљ хоща ант эвтатаљ, – акайн ястас.

Варасљаљ вощлаха ёваљсаљљы, щи юшљ хуват, апщеӈаљаљ пеља няхман, сэм пелкаљ нямрэмаман, ныкљы нёпиељ хоща руӈкас. Воиељ туп љаљтман ешащас. Ин љув вутан, торнаӈ кељаљ войљ хонаӈ патаља лукемасљы, мевљаљ шома ярсаљљы. Кимет кељ шупаљ курӈаљаљ шома ярсаљљы. Щаљта љув вуты шушас, кељ ољнаљ апщенаљаља масљы.

– Я, муй! Сухтаљэв воев, тата хун хайљэв! – Юхур аяљта сухтасљы войљ. Апщенаљљаљ юрн, муй кем щём тайсатан, кељ сухтасљан.

– Аљ тэрматыятан, воев шакаптаљэв. Аяљтыена вуты таљљэв. Рома уљатан.

Воељ ищи куш намн вощлахан вуратыяс, сэмӈаљаљ вољљы вуртыя ювамӈан, вощлах онтасан. Елљы такан куш уљты љанхаса. Вантсаљљы хун, муй вура љонас. Аяљта, рома кељн таљман, вощлахаљн ёнрапман эсљапса. Ин щаљта мохиљаљн таканшак, сорашак сухтаса, воељ нох љояпты ванта кум ант ат шитас. Ешавуљ сорам лот унты нярэмасэљ. Воељ мохты нох навармас. Љоямтас па,ељ ёхи анкармас, амуй сормаљ ёхтас, амуй љыљаљ сохнас. Няврэмат, туп воељ вуты сухтасэљ, љув хощайљ хухаљмасат. Нёпиељ па вуты, унт пеља навармас. Щита иљ љояс. Љояс, љояс, щаљта тарнатас па, няврэмат вощлахан лап рыйсайт. Щаљта щи мохиљаљ няхты питсат, щимащ мољты отшам вой таймељ.

Ешавуљ, хољыена унта љоӈксат. Нёта канкшты, нохар сэӈкты. Юхур ун юх шуп љэщатмаљ, нохар сэӈктыя. Нохар юхљаљ тэљан йиӈаљаљ нох тахармељ. Ун нохар шупљаљ ухљаљ ин там унты сормељ ныља. Вољљы вуртыя ювмељ. Акайн ун нохар юх пунља љояс, юх шупаљн курљ эљты такан рэскасљы. Ин щаљта щи нохар шупат ох патыя рыйты питсат. Кураӈ воељ мет хувашак навармас, няврэмӈан ищиељ хухаљмастан, љыљљан шавиман. Йи пуш рэскаман, хољна па аршак нохар иљ рыйљ. Акайн вуты, унт пеља шушмас, ястаман, йи лотн љуљн ат омасљатан, нохарљан акаттан юпиян. Нохар сэм ат сэмиљтан. Сорьёхан похие осхиељ пиљн увман, ешащман нохар акатты питщастан.

– Ма нохрэм мет ун!

– Анта! Ма нохрэм уншак! – сыяŋа увман, ешащсатан нявремŋан. Хув кураŋ воиян нохар еша эпсантас, щиŋанща пуŋља манс, па иљ кератљыяс.

– Муй ям уятсатан уŋхан нохар хоща љув ай љухасŋаљљаљ. Такиљыи увљатан па ешащљатан, щит муй љэтот.

Таŋха такан метс. Вощлах кут муй каш вер уљ, самаљ такан манс. Похлэнки ай эвие пиљн хољна хув нохар кашман ешащсатан. Муй нохар уятљатан, щикем хирана шавапљаљљан. Торн кутн, варс кутн пуратман, нохрат хољыена акатсаљљан. Щаљта юхшуп эљты омассатан па нохар сэм сэмиты питсатан. Унт љопас љэвпас шек умащ уљмаљ. Сэмия па сэмия. Нумн тута, унт патыйн акайн юх шуп пора порайн щащиљыты сыйљ щащас. Нэмољты эљты љын ат хурыљтан, акайн ванан, войн тата щи ољман ешащаљ. Пора порайн эљаљ туп аљ тарантыяљ. Пунљаљ тохи вощлаха сормељ. Щит ун вер антом. Щаха нох питљат. Вощлаха љоŋљан ки, хой ат паљтапаљ, хоят хољна вуты киљты вољан ант верытаљ. Порайн охаљ нох аљмиљљы, нявремат пеља аŋкартыман. Щаљта па иљ вояпља.

Ешавуљ акайн нык, љын хощайн ёхтас. Љанкар эљты хуљам хир тахармамаљ. Апщеŋаљаљ мохты вантты питщастан, амуйн акайн хирљаљ тэваљмаљ. Кат хираљн – нёта. Хуљмет хираљн – нохар. Љын хиран шупљ унты туп ёхтас. Акайн па таљаŋ хуљам хир.

– Мин хирэмн па вољљы таљ, куш кепа мин нохарљаман таљан тэљн акатсаљљаман.

– Ям арат щи акатман йи юх эљты, ма вет юх эљты пайтам нохарљам. Нын щи каркамŋан. Кураŋ войн муйн ямас кум шитас щутщаты. Ин шай инщемаљув па, ёхи манљув.

Щи ясŋат онтасан, нявремŋан мохты самљан вохты питсайтан. Унанкан хир љыпия анкармастан. Нянь, щумах љэты омассат. Ям љоват нянь шуп хув кураŋ воиеља мешапсат, љув там хатљ мет метам вой.

Йи матты хатљ, етн, иљ ољтэљ ељпиян, акайн љаварт потар ољаŋ вус.

– Аљансахат аљŋашак нох киљљув. Хув кураŋ воев унта туљэв.

– Муя па унта љувељ тутыя? – апщеŋаљаљ нох навармастан, – утн љув тапаљ. Хольща љувељ щаха каншљэв!

– Воев унтан сэма питам вой. Унт мувљ щит љув хотаљ. Щита љув анкељ уљ, похаљ љављасты метс, иљампа.

Щимащ ясаŋ потартас Юхур анта туп апщеŋаљаља, љувељ мет щаль ус воиељ. Щи љоват войљ хоща утљас па, ищи матты щит љув нbackgroundврэмаљ.

– Нёпиев энмас. Уна йис. Ин сусн войт љув юшељ хуват, кармас кут эљты, унта манљат. Воев, аŋкељ пиљн щита щи уйтантаљ.

– Мин па хой пиљн ёнтты питљаман? – апщеŋаљљаљ нюхмастан.

– Љувељ утн ямшак, хоят пиљн торас, – щиŋанща машьяя ювман, Юхур ким этас.

Щи куш љув уятљаљљы, воеља утн уљты ям, љащкамшак, щит љув муваљ. Туп ай няврэм иты нёпиељ пиљн ант љанхаса катна манты. Љув ищи апщиеŋаљаљ иты, ёнтты пиљ каншас таŋха. Љуŋ сыс самаљ воиељ хоща тохи карљас. Ищи матты войљ апщие юкана йис. Щи тумпиян войљ эљты шек хурыман ус, ульня хоятатн пошканан аљт эсаљља. Хоят хоща утљам вой, паљтаплы кашаŋ хоят ещаљт манљ. Утн љув туп сэма питс. Энмас па хоятат кутн. Аŋкељн кашаŋ хатљ потартылља:

– Воиен энамаљ, уна йиљ, щаха хоятат хоща утаљтаљ юпиян, унта хун љэщаљаљ. Ун вой шики хоятат хоща ант љэпаљ. Оŋтан вой торас вераљ, љов хун. Унта ин туты мосљ, хољна ай уљтаљн.

Унаŋканан няврэмŋан щи куш поякљайтан, љын хатљ хуват сэмыйиŋкан сэман шушиљыљтан. Войн щаль. Питљор эвие хољљаты вољыйс туп, хун љын унаŋкан пиљн сапаљ кељ ёнтты омассатан.

– Сапаљ кељ воева шек мосаљ, хоятн ант моштаља. Ёш вой мосаŋ пошканан ант эсаљља. Вурты нуй љувеља ант мосаљ. Восты нуй эљты кељн ётљэман. Лыпат хоям хорпи нуйљ эљты па ханшийн ёнты. Унаŋкељн эвие ханшийн эватса. Ин щитљаљ ёнтман љув пайљы ям хув кут опсас.

– Ханшиљам ин сус лыптат хорпия ныясты питљат, войн хољна ант шияљаљайт, – нумасас эвие.

– Унаӈки! – ивевн унаӈкан инщасман ешащсатан няврэмӈан, – нёпиев па утн хота ољты питљ, акаев хашап ёљн хащаљ.

– Па љув ёљан щи уљты питљ. Щита аӈкељ уљ. Љув хуван ванан похаљ љаваљљаљљы.

– Хотљ па муй хорпи?

– Хотаљ? – еша ронс унаӈкан, – хотљ, нови сахаӈ сумат юх эљты верман уљ. Каман мољщанан хоп юх, нак юх, вутан нохар юх эљты верман уљ. Ертан ант посыља, вотн ат пољља.

– Яна ям, хошам, хорамаӈ хот аӈкељ таймаљ, – амтатљыман Питљор эвие ястас.

– Ољты па хота питљ?

– Ољты ураӈан аӈкељан ваншийн љэщатса, осам хирљ нётаян, муй туӈкан, ухаљ варсан понља. Щимащ осам хир эљты ољаљ, нын уртыян пиљн љувеља уљма питљатан.

– Па щиты ки…, аӈкељ щи хорпи ям хот ки тайљ…, – туса интпаљан ёнтасман, хољна еша щаль войљ эсаљты верн, ястас Питљор эвие, – щиты ки муӈ љувељ унта туљэв.

– Ям щи! Љув унт вой хоты, аӈкељ пиљн љувељ уљты мосаљ. Ищи љув хорпи љухас утн уятаљ. Нёпиян ханты, хоят ясаӈан нын пиљанан потартты ант верытаљ. Љув ищи марэмаља љухасљаљ, аӈки таклы. Ищи потрэматы љаӈхаља.

Сапаљ кељаљ ёнттаљн, унаӈкељ, мет рэньљы сохам каншас. Сора щаха кељаљ ат тохнамтас.

– Сапаљ кељаљ тохаљ ки, мет ям, унашак йитаљ кемн, щита кељаљн шакаттаља. Љув сора энамаљ, сапаљ кељаљ ая хащљ.

Аљаӈсахат нёпие мохиљаљ шек аљӈа, най туп хутљаты питс, нох киљсат. Ким этмељн торн, лыптат эљты ат йиӈаљ хољна ољаљ. Няврэм ун сэмьйиӈк иты мува щёшӈаљтам хорпи, найљ сэм ещаљт хорамљыман волисат. Няврэмӈан аяљтыена, ат йиӈаљ ант ат иљ ронты ураӈан шушсатан. Лыптат ищи матты росэӈ сак понман хорамљыљат хоты. Щи хорпи хорам мувељ аљаӈсахат уљмаљ. Хув кураӈ воиян хоты наварман ныкљы манс, љувељ росы хоща вер антом. Љув навармам манам юшљ хуват вутаӈ сорам юш хащас. Намн воељ ищи хопа љэљсэљ, ёшљаљ, курљаљ иљ ярсаљљаљ, нык ант ат навармаљ. Питљор эвие

Соръёхан похие пиљн ищи хопа љэљсатан. Хопа љэљман кемн, па щи марэмастан, войн унта тутан юпиян, хой пиљан ёнтљатн. Мантан хуват щи вощхисљан, щи вощхисљан љухсыян. Хув кураӈ воиян туп ох пушхаљн кератман нняврэмӈан сэмьйиӈк аљ нёљэмияљ.

– Наӈ аљ паља утн, муӈ наӈен аӈкен хоща туљэв. Аӈкенан мохты шияљаљайн па нын хотана ёхи манљатан.

Ай нняврэмӈан щимащ вера ищи такан эваљман устан, унаӈканан ястасайтан хоты. Ешавуљ воњљы ёрэмаман хорпи, хољта пеља манљат, воянан нёљэматы кутн, щикем ляхаӈ хорпи. Няхман, каман щирн ёнтты питсатан войн пиљн. Хопељ юпиян най љуйљаљ, хоп иљпи эљты рыйты йиӈк сэмљаљ пиљн ёнтман, љый юпељан нюхљасыяс. Утн, Юхур, нняврэмат па нёпие нох вуты киљмељ юпиян, па щи хорам мува ликапсат. Пащар юхељ ищи хорпи вурты сак понмаљ хорпи, ат йиӈкан иса лап паркатам. Ищи матты волиты нови кев шукан, сак юкана хорамљам. Щимащ кев нэнат ивевн ов пунља, мохиљаљ ойељ, нуптэљ ураӈан потамтыљэљ. Хув кураӈ воељ пащар юх шияљамаљ кемн, амуй таӈха рых вощты вутщияс, амуй тохи нэрасты љанхаса, тохи ниншапмаљ кемн ерта ювмаљ хорпи. Ин юхаљ эљты щи арат ат йиӈкан рыйса па, ёхљы нняврэмат хоща паљтамаман хухаљмас. Еша хухатљыман, ун вутаӈ лыпат кутн ат йиӈк куштэљ уятмаљ, щитљ ёхи инщемасљы. Љувељ иса каш, унт хорасат шияљаты.

– Ма уятљэм, муя вутаӈ лыпат хоща ат йиӈкаљ ара йиљ. Ат йиӈк сэмљаљ аиет, – нюхмас Питљор эвие, – яха хатэмаљат, ун йиӈк лота йиљат. Унаӈкем ястыяс, Ун Асэв ищиты, кашан сойм, ёхан эљты йиӈкан овља. Щи ураӈан Ун Асэв ун йиӈкаӈ. Йиӈкаљ ант хољаљыяљ, атаӈ хатљ овља. Нняврэмӈан љын щиранан каман вер эљты шитаман потрэмастан, муй вер эљты уятљатан, ванта.

– Ма ищи хуљљысам унаӈкем эљты, ешавуљ юх лыптат вошамн хойтэљ юпиян иљ рыйљат, – Соръёхан похие ястас. Сумат юх лыпатљаљ воњљы хоямат, таӈха атаљн ищки ус.

– Ака! Хольща щи арат йиӈк питас? Мољхатљ ант щи ертас! – ищмастан нняврэмӈан.

– Па там ат йиӈк ат уљ. Етн соймат эљты пошам охаљмаљ нырља. Атаљн, патлам кутн сэмљы Пошам икен тата таӈха шушиљыяс. Морам пунаŋ кувщаљ нох хошкаман, ант ат потљa. Љув эљтайљ щи арат ат йиŋк хащас. Щахашак найљ этталь юпиян, ат йиŋкаљ сорљ, наяљн ёхи инщемаљайт.

Хув кураŋ воиељ па щи юхат кута љонас, ин па сумат юх лыпат таŋха нярэматы вутщияс. Нумаљта па щи йиŋкан щёшемаса. – Муй арат йиŋк, – таŋха, љув нумасаљ, хар тахая хухаљмаман.

Щаљта Юхур войљ сапаљ кељ хоща кељ ярас, апщеŋаљаљ хоп љыпийн китмаљ юпиян, войљ пиљн унта шушмас. Шек хув ахота љув утн яŋхас. Ешавуљ ат йиŋкаљ сорас, сус, нэмољты ат хошмаљты найљ хувн ванан турам хуват яŋхты питмаљ, нявремŋан љын щиранан ёнттан эљты. Питљор эвие па Сорљёхан похие пиљн нянь шук йиŋка парнаљман ешащсатан, нялк љапатман. Ай сортат ищи уна ювмељ. Љын ёнтман, љупан йиŋк эљты вораскаљљан, ай сортат пуŋља манљат, ешавуљ па хоп пуŋља ущљат. Љын ёнттан эљты акайн ёхтас. Машьяйн хопљ нык поткасљы, юраŋ моторaљ сухтасљы, ёхљы пеља манты юшаљ вусљы. Нявремŋан, љув веншаљ пеља аŋкармаман кемн, нэмољты вер эљты инщасты ант питсатан. Акайн венш патлам хорпи, веш мораммаљ муйн йи лота сухтамаљ. Муя таљтахийн акайн кетамты. Мољты мосаљ ки, љув ястаљ. Йи хатљ хун ияха уљљат, муй мосаљ верты иса уятљэљ. Хун потарты, хун машьяйн еша омасты. Акайн, мотор катаљман, сывасн омасаљ. Љувељ ељљы манты юш туп ныља. Љын љуп катаљты лотанан акайн ещаљт омасљатан, щишн манты юш патан, унт пеља, туп ныља. Щишн, хун љын такан щалыты питсатан, акайн хољна ољаŋ сыс хащшак ант паљтамас.

– Кураŋ вой! Кураŋ воев! Хув кураŋ воиев! Ванты са Ака!

Пан хуват такан наварман унт эљты этмас воељ. Кутн вощлаха љоŋэмиман, кущайљаљ юпиян, тэрмаљаман, наварман йис.

– Аŋкељ хоща љув таŋха ат љаŋхаља уљты! – такан увман, ешащсатан нявремŋан. – Аŋкељ эљты хонтамаљ. Мун пиљэвн љув уљты љаŋхаља!

Хув кураŋ воиељ щи хатљ ёхи щи тусэљ.

Таљ Турам каш хатљат

Питљор эвие йи матты тарам ищки хатљатан шек кашаŋа йис. Амуй таŋха хув каман хухатљыяс, хощты мушн иляпса. Љэтотн сараљыља, ант љэљ. Ишни пеља туп вантыяљ, љухасŋаљаљ камн хухатљыљтан, љув па ёљан ољаљ. Вољљы иса кашљыя ювман ољаљ. Ишниљаљ вотасн лап тувамт. Нэмољты камн ант ныља. Аŋкељ ястаљ, каман шек ищки, љаљты шув еŋка потља. Таљ турам питщамаљ эљты, еша хутљыяљ, щаљта яљпа па патлаљ. Най имен ищи хотљ эљты воља ŋ ким этљытаљ антом, ин љув иса курљ аљљыман, ёљан омасаљ хошмаљтыман. Љувеља ищи камн, тарм ищкийн атам, мохты потља, щи онтасан, ким этмитаљ кемн, веншаљ вољљы вуртыя ныясаљ. Мохет пеља аŋкармаљ, муй љув верљат? Хой курљ аљљыяљ, хой тут юх унт эљты аљљыяљ? Мосаŋ хой потса? Аŋкармитаљ юпиян, яљпа ёхи, хошам хотаља љоŋемаљ. Еŋка потам Ас шоппи хоты, сорни тынаŋ хотљ хатљаљн яма ныља. Ас папелак вуртата сухтатман уљ, таŋха курљ такан, хошмат аљљыљљы. Ант ат потља. Љув ханематаљ кемн, ким этмаљ тыљащ шуп. Таљ хуват љув щутщаты кум ант шитаљ. Хатљ кутап юпиян ким навармаљ. Љув юпељн, ешавуљ муй арат ар хус тураман нох тахарман тайља, хољыена каљыя хутљаљат, хоята яŋхты манты юш яљман.

Питљор эвие щикуш ёшиељ ишни пеља таљљыљљы, юрљ ант тармаљ, па ёшљ тохи ант ёхатаљ. Аŋкељн па унаŋкељн щи арат мавŋ љэтотан омасса па, тумтак ус ки, щи эпљан мављаљ мохты љуљн ёхи љавемасљы. Ин вољљы кашљы. Аӈкељн пора порайн портонан мийљыља, щи вер эљты Питљор эвие мохты моштасљы. Аӈкељ нэпек шукие эљты портон нялы љыпия шошемаљ, шанша карэмаман, эљты па саккараӈ компот йиӈкан амармаљљы па ясталь:

– Ванта муй хорпи ям саккараӈ љэтотат. Яблока пулт, амуй мољты вонщапат, щи хорпи саккараӈат па эпљаӈат. Еша тахты куш кепа инщемия.

Питљор эвие, нэмољты верљы, таљ тахийн ољаљ хоты, рупата љувељ антом онтасан, уӈљаљ пелки пушмиљљы, портонаљ уӈља аљ шошемиља. Љув па компот пеља вантман, каман щира нумасыяљ – ахоты щи арат хошап юхн энамљат. Щи љоват љаварт хошап эљты, юх нувљаљ аты морэмаљат. Тащ хошап энамаљ, рущљан туп нииншамтыљат, па саккараӈ умащ љэтот љэва па љэва.

– Анки! Ант мосаљ манэм саккараӈ вонщап, мия манэм потам йиӈк. Љонщи ветраен эљты амарма.

– Ант рахаљ, щаха леккар хота понљайн.

– Антом ки, потам мисьйиӈк ай поталые шуката! – щикем потам от љанхаљайм!

– Ант рахаљ! Леккар имийн щаха кимантак ляватљайман.

Камаљта ёхи Юхур акайљ љонемас. Љув юпељан, хатытљыман ольпаӈ хотхар эљты кураӈ воиељ ёхи љоӈемас. Хот кутап унты туп шитас шушты, иљ хотхара ољамтас, курљаљ япсыена иљшак ханятсаљљы, љув иљпеља. Еша уљман, яљпа нох вуратс, тупайљаљн курӈаљтыман, кущайљ пуӈља љояс.

– Муй хорпи нељаӈ! Ин хоты ма ям љэтотљам холыена ёхи ворљаљљы, – Питљор эвие љув щираљн нумасман пайљы ољман хащас, – манэма нэмољты ат хайљ.

Хув кураӈ войн компот хошапт холыена эпсатсаљљы. Ант рахсат таӈха љувеља, тортатљыман пуӈља карэмас. Питљор эвие ёшљ нёљэмас. Щаљта япсыена љояс па ёш патљ ляхеӈа холыя нёљсаљљы.

– Щиты ки, ма щаха йии пелак саккараӈ љэтотэм наӈен љапатталљэм. Щи мољты компот яна эпљаӈ.

Кураӈ воиељ хоты туп овљ пеља аӈкармияљ, ахун ов пуншаталь, ким наварматы ураӈан. Питљор эвие яма уятљаљљы, ин акайљ уртыељ пиљн там порайн љовљан ищаљтаты матсатан. Кураŋ войн па љувељ каш ураŋан ёљн хайсаљљан. Соръёхан похие там хатљ љув куща, утща љов љоŋља омасман нык наварман манас. Етна пеља, хун акайн хољап эљты ёхи ёхатаљ. Љув хуљам хоят љоват ищаљтаты яŋхљат. Љын љов хот љоŋља хуŋхљатан, нумаљта љов шанша навармаљтан. Љован пуŋљашак шушмаљ ки, ёвра иљ љонща керытљыљтан. Питљор эвие хоты акаяљн љов шанша опсаљља. Соръёхан похие яљпа љов хот љоŋља хуŋхаљ, па ипуш навармияљ. Акайн ољна шушаљ ай љоваљ пиљн омлэп унты. Љын па љув юпељан ун љов шаншан манљатан, уŋкељ катаљман. Ипуш акайн Эрапта эљты вуљэŋ ухаљн ёхтас, щиŋанща мохты туп шай инщты кум шитас, ун яйљ хоща манс. Тумељ кев эљты там пелка касаљмаљ. Ин щиŋанща няврэмŋан љын щиранан омлэп унты љов шанша љэљман матсатан. Љовљан тэрматман щи навармастан. Рэп иљпиян Питљор эвие роман иљ ракнас љоваљ эљты, уŋкељаљ катаљты таŋха ант шитсаљљы. Красавкайљ љув эљтайљ хащ ант навармаман, омлэпљ унты љув ёхтас. Соръёхан похие щи нstriкс осхиељ иљ раканмаљ эљты.

– Љов љоŋаљн хољна омасты ант хошљан, хота па наварты, наŋ љуљн ёљан омассан, љовљам ма щи йиŋка тутљыты вертљаљљам!

Питљор эвие машьяйн аплак кутн хащас. Љов љоŋља ищипа ант верытаљ хуŋхты. Ёхљы, рэп љонља љув курљаљн шушас. Уртыељ па љов љонљаљн омасман ёхи манас. Кураŋ войљ па, ищи таŋха няхман, ипуша куща нэŋаљ нёљаљн поткаман навратљыяљ. Нёпиељ ёнтты љаŋхаса, Питљор эвие хољљап сурн уљ хоты, нумасаљ, воиељн нэман љонща поткаља. Питљор эвие войљ ељ куш поткаљљы, тумељн ёхљы поткаља. Щиты поткатман, эвие вољљы аплак кута поткасљы.

– Мана таљта ељ, аљ потканта, – такан хољљаты питс эвилэŋки, – наŋ манэм аплака, љонща поткасэн. Ма наŋ пиљэнан па ант питљам ёнтты. Утща ёнта, – хољљас эвие.

Хув кураŋ воиељн ант шитса нох куртты. Эвие щита щи аплак кутн ољман хащас. Ешавуљ нёпиељ, куртасман, ёхи, Соръёхан похиељ юпиян хухаљмас.

Нумн, Турамн тыљащ пелак ищи нях вешн эвие пеља вантман љояс. Љувељ таŋха ищи щаљь ус хољљаман хащам ай эвие. Еша хољљап сур эльты воԓыман, Питԓор эвие хомта, шанш вураԓа керытԓыяс, нохԓы турам пеԓа вантман. Хошам саԓтам вайԓаԓн, пушԓ шовар сохн пуштам сахаԓн куш таԓаӈ хатԓ ԓонщ эльты керытԓыя, ант потԓа. Нумн щи арат хус тахартам па. Аԓ волиԓат. Кураӈ вой хусԓаԓ ищиты нумн ԓойтэԓ ныԓа.

– Амуя па воием нюхаԓсэм. Муй атам ԓув манэм верас. Нумаԓта ин ԓув ԓуӈхаԓ ма пеԓаем вантаԓ, па нумасаԓ, муй хорпи ма атам эвие. Па ԓув ищи манэм муй арат пуш ԓонща поткисԓы! – пойкащман нумасаԓ Питԓор эвие. Ар хус пеԓа вантман, ай эвие номасан ёхатса:

– Ма ԓуԓн щи арат хорам каԓы хус эльты унаӈкема саклопс каратсам. Анта унаӈкема. Унаӈкем ант кашащаԓ, анкем па хорасаӈ. Ԓувеԓа волиты сакпаԓ шек ԓуԓн рахас. Аӈкеԓ щи хорпи саклопс хорасаӈ нопсаԓн ватман, эвилэӈки воԓԓы амтас, ищиматты яна сакпаԓан аӈкеԓ каратсаԓԓы. Питы лавм хорпи сэмпи, картэӈ сэвпи аӈкеԓ ин мет хорамаӈ питԓ нэӈат кутн! Питԓор эвие щи номасԓаԓ эльты нох навармас, кура ԓоямтас, ԓонщԓаԓ паркатсаԓԓы, вайӈаԓаԓ нох сухтасԓы, па ёхи хухаԓман манас. Тыԓщаԓ такан юшԓ альман, турам хуват ԓув юпеԓн ищи хухаԓман манас.

Там хатԓ иԓампа уртыем амтатԓыяԓ, утща ԓовн омасаԓ, ма па кашаӈ. Щи номасԓаԓ кеман Соръёхан похие ёхи ԓоӈемас. Ԓув ищи утща марэмаса. Каман ёнтты хоят ант тайԓ. Нёпиеԓ, ԓув ов пушмаԓ кемн ким навармас, ԓовԓаԓ хоща манс. Ёнттыя. Уртыеԓ, ԓув щираԓн еша тахты ёнтас. Осхиеԓ инщассаԓԓы:

– Параник наӈен мосаԓ?

Питԓор эвие охаԓн туп вотэмас. Ԓэты кашԓ антом ус. Аӈкеԓ иԓампа мисԓаԓ пусты манс.

– Наӈ манэм потам йиӈк амарма. Ԓонщи путат эльты. Потам йиӈк йинщты шек ԓаӈхаԓаям.

Похлэӈки амтас, моԓты вер ԓувеԓа ищи ликмас. Ԓонщи путԓ эльты таԓаӈ умпи потам йиӈк амармас. Осхиеԓ охаԓ эльты нох нётсаԓԓы аԓамты. Умпеԓ эльты ԓоԓам ԓонщ, потам йиӈкан инщаԓтасԓы. Щи хорпи умащ потам йиӈк уԓмаԓ. Мав хорпи! Питԓор эвие хащ умпи тэԓ йиӈк таԓаӈ таԓаӈ тэԓн ант хорэмасԓы. Щи кутн аӈкеԓ камаԓта ёхи ԓоӈемас. Ёшаԓн мурхи ан аԓэмамаԓ. Потам мурахԓаԓ хуљ вой пиљн љыљатмаљ. Апщељ, потам няр йиŋкпи умпи пиљн шияљаман, эвељ эљты пуŋља партсаљљы. Леккар щи кутн ёхи ант љоŋемас, ошиљыљљы няврэмŋан. Щи потам йиŋкаљ йинщмаљ юпиян, Питљор эвие ешавуљ тумтака йис. Яма ювмаљ юпиян, муй арат компот ус, холљыена уртыељ пиљн ёхи љухаљсаљљан. Кураŋ войн эљты вољљы ёрэмасљан.

Унт мув нарасъюх сыйт

– Хаљыват порвой каншты унта манљув. Хой хув ољты питљ, щи хоятэв унта патн ант вуљэв, – Акайн ољтахаяљა иљ ољты љэщатыяс. Љув ки иљ ољаљ, ай отђан ищи ољты верн уљ. Акайн иљ ољтаљ юпиян, унађкан монщ хољна ант монщиљыяљ.

– Метам ху, еша куш кепа ат щутщаљ.

Пощтуљ няврэмђан иљ ољты ант куш кашащсатан, туп унађканан муйин ястасайтан, щи пеља хуљатты мосаљ. Ант љађхаман, ољтаха сахљан нык сухтасљан. Аяљта ёхлы пеља авашман иљ љэщатыстан. Па хоты верты, акайн нох куратты ант рахаљ, љув хатљ хуват рупитас, такан метс.

Товийн, унт љыпийн шек ям. Тови нояђ хатљатан, Най имен љуйљаљ кашађ юх вощхиљљы. Щи онтасан, унт љыпиян ищи матты нови тут нох хатщаса. Юхлаљ ищи матты љуђ пора эльты нумасман, нувљаљ каљы востыя ювмељ. Кашађ нув най пеља таљасаљ. Сумат юхлаљ хољна аплак кутн љойљат, ищи матты хорамађ нови сахн љуматлыман. Ёнтам ханшиљаљн кутљаљн ишкащљат. Хой ханши мет хорасађ, мет тусађ. Маты юх там хатљ мояђ хоятн шияљаља?

Йис нохар юхлаљ аљ щи ађкармиљат сумат юхт пеља, љув ищи кум ант шитљат. Љуђ пора унты љэпасљаљ ништыљљаљ. Сус унты нохар энмаљты мосаљ. Щаха каман вой – љађкет, нёхас войт, хођхр, нохар љэты нэђен, хоятэн, хољыена љуђан нохар каншты питљат. Тови пора сора хащљ, љуӈа йиљ, аӈкарматы кум ант шитљан, муй арат пищ. Тащ нохар ат энамаљ, войт љэљљы хащљат. Наӈк юхљаљ, хошам љонщи мољщаӈљаљ нох эӈхапмељ, хуватэљн нярты љойљат. Нувљаљ хошмаљман, най ещаљт аӈкармиљат. Катра там юх сураља, сэварматы ураӈан, ху хоят ёшаљ туп љаям вуты верытас. Нэ хоятата ун ем, там юх сэварты. Катра ики хуљ юх љэпасљаљ хоты вољљы иса восты порвойн лап энмамт. Љув хоты мощ икет иты, порвояӈ сэмљаљ тупан нох мир пеља вантыман уљљат. Порвой пунан лап энмамт хоты. Љув хоты љављасман уљљат, хун пунаӈ порвойљаљ вуљэтн, муй кураӈ воятн нох нярэмаљайт. Муйкем пирщемам хуљ юхаљ, щикем аршак порвойн энмам.

Найљ, амтатљыман, тови хатљат ёхатмељ кашн, кашаӈ юх нув иљпия љоӈемияљ. Ай вой хот љыпеља хољна љоӈемияс, аӈкармиясољты кущайљ пеља, нох куратсаљљы. Тумељ ким навармас, мољты љэтот шук каншман унт хуват хухаљмас. Унт љыпиян ищи матты емаӈ катра нарасъюх ар совљ нэрман, каман щищки сыйн унт мув сыйљаслы. Кураӈ вой эљты верам нарасъюх љонљаљ ар сыйљ хува щащаљ. Най имеља арыяљ, хоты таљ хуват, тарам ищкийн унт войт усат. Най имељ ищи таљ хуват атаӈ хатљ хот љыпељн омасман марэмаса, ищкийн потман. Ин щишн кашаӈ вой пиљн ёнтман ёшљаљ ёнтљат. Ахота макла имен уваљтас, щи сый эљты ин, нячврэмат хув кураӈ воиељ паљтамаман, ељ навармас, паљљаљ нох аљамман. Ат хуват ант ољам макла имен ищи хоятат эљты паканман, тохљаљ иљпия иљ ханемас. Љувељ муй вер яӈхты, манты мохет пеља. Љув хоты нови сахаљн таљ хуват хун па потса. Љохан унта ёхтам мохет сыяӈа щиркман шушсат порвой кашман. Хой хатмиман, хой иљ ракныман шушсат. Юхур љохљаљ вой сохн сухтаман онтасан, шитама кер љонщ эљты манљат, ястаљат: «Шитам, шитам». Нячврэм љохт па такан щирӈаљсат, ищи матты увман ешащљат: «Щирк-щирк, щурк-щурк». Хув кураӈ воиељ па хой ишн љонща рохнемияљ, кер љонщан ант щиљта эљты катаљты, па љонемияљ, па љонемияљ. Љув љонща љонемитаљ кемн, нарасъюх сыйт ищи аљ таратыљат. Мохет љохн шушиљыљат хоты, љув па љохлы. Антом ки Юхурн љуљн няљ љохн верса. Щи арат љох кутн мет љуљн курљаљ иљ тахрапсат.

Ољаŋан унта ёхтам мояŋ хоятат порвой хуљ юхт иљпиян сухтысат, туп кураŋ воељ ивољапа торас верс. Љув эпљаŋ љэтотаљ нярэмаман, иса торастыяс. Няврэмат пуŋља поткаљљы, љув аршак порвойŋ лота љоямтаљ. Няврэмŋан такан, сыяŋа увман, войн ељ нюхаљљаљљан, љув па нэман вана йиљ. Питљор эвие иљта порвойљ сухатмаљ кемн, акайљ пеља ястас, љувељ нуманшак уљты нувљаља опсаљтыя. Љув нумасаљ, войљ эљты щи кемн хонтаљ. Акаяљн юх нув эљты нохшак опсапса. Кураŋ войљ, кущайљ опсам нуваљ эљты пекљаљн порвой сухтыты питс. Ин эвие нувљ тяттиты такан питс. Питљор эвие щи љоват такан увты питс, утн уљты вой мир иљампа хољыена нох куратсаљљы.

– Мана таљта ељ, ошиљыљы вой! Акаем хоща мет эпљаŋ порвой энамаљ! Ма юхемн атам порвой энаммаљ. – Уŋљаља порвой лукемас, еша љухљапсаљљы, ким ляксасљы. – Пфу! Вощрэм, ахоты наŋ тамащ вощрэм љэтот љухаљљан.

Кураŋ войљ хоты юхаљ эљты век пуŋља ат шушаљ. Муй кем такан кущайљ увас, щикем љув таканшак юх нувљ сухтысљы. Вай нёљаљ эљты иљ нярэмаман. Љув таŋха нумасаљ, ай кущайљ љувељ вохљаљљы нёттыя, щи онтасан юх нувљ сухтыљљы. Ешавуљ Питљор эвие иљ щи кер љонщ эљты ракнас. Кураŋ воиељ мохты Соръёхан похие хоща хухаљмас, щита па мосаљ вантты, муй ёх кущайљ вераљ. Ешавуљ щи пелак эљты ув сыйт щащты питсат:

– Мана таљта ељ! Ма хирэм хољна таљ, муя торастыљан, хун ма кум шитљам порвой сухатты. Муя наŋ отшам, туŋа щира мана наŋ порвой љухља. Муя торастаљан! Муя ма љохем эљты љойсан?

Ята!! Щи пелак эљты љох шукаљам сый щащас. Питљор эвие уртыељ хоща хухаљман манс. Соръёхан похие, љув ёхатмаљн, шукаљам љохљ туп ёшаљн катљас. Љохаљ яха поныљыман, хољљаман ешащас. Ин љув ёхљы манты юшаљн куран туп верытаљ шушты.

– Муй хорпи каркам! Ай пиљыен љохаљ шукатмен! – шаншаљ эљты вощхемасљы, вана ёхтам Юхур, кураŋ воиељ.

– Хоты ма ёхи манљам? – йи љохн хащам Соръёхан похие ниŋхарљаман ястас. Љув кер љонщ эљты ељ ёхи наварман ешащас.

– Ёхи хоты ёхатљув, кер љонщ хуват кураŋ войн хољна верытаљ шушты, нын па кен хоятыеŋан. Йи љох хоща муй ун вер, – шукатам љохљ вантыман ястас Юхур.

– Ёхи ёхатљув, яљап љох омасљув верты. Наӈ па манэм нётљан яљап љох верты, – апщиељ ох патљ эљты вощхиман, Юхур апщеӈаљаљ пиљн потартман љойс. – Хув кураӈ воев тупайљаљ љаварт ураӈан љохен шукатсаљљы. Хирљув муйн кеныет, таљ порвой, муй љаварт тайљ. Я, муй ёхи шушмаљув? – љаӈкраља кат хиртэљ порвой кат пелак сахат юватсаљљы, кељн яха ярман.

– Ахун кум шитас акаемн щи арат порвой сухатты, мин хирљаман вољљы таљт? – нумассатан апщеӈаљљаљ. Аљаӈсахат иты љув хољыена ёхи шушмасат. Ин хоты воељ тарамља мосты љэтотаљн. Торн љув ат љаӈхаља, таљ нянь, па мисьйиӈк. Сољ хољна вохаљ. Кашаӈ кураӈ вой, акайн ястас, таљн порвой љухаљљат.

Кимет таља йис, кураӈ воељ хоятат кутн уљтаљ. Ипуш акаян па щи унта актащиты питс, кураӈ войн утн хайты ураӈан. Ун керљонщ тыљащан акайн войљ пиљн Вуљыкурт унты матсатан. Хув мува таӈха матсатан, акайн патлатаљ кемн туп ёхи ёхтас. Унаӈкан похаљ љапатман, ељ ёхи хухатљыманшак шушиљыяс. Пут тэљ нёхи кавармаљ, ин щи путљ вуты хонс, нyврэмљаљ љапатман. Юхур машьяйн, питы веншан љэты опсас. Питљор эвие уртыељ пиљн ищи љув пељайљ сэм иљта аӈкармистан. Иса хољыена машьяйн омастэљ эљты унаӈкан такан нюхмас:

– Муй сэмьйиӈк акатман омасљаты! Кураӈ войн нын эљтан хољта манљ?

Акайн веш мохты каљыя, новия ховемас. Ищи матты нэмољты войљ хоща вер ант тайљ, шайљ инщман хащас. Ай отӈаљаљ па наварман кимљы хухаљмастан. Хув кураӈ воиељ такан метмаљ, ай кущайӈаљаљ эљты нянь вохман ешащас.

Там хатљ па акайн хољљам вешн хот пуӈаљн опсас. Такан метмаљ. Юрљы иса хащмаљ. Сойм пелак эљты ай хопн ёхатмаљ ныља Соръёхан похие. Љув ищи охаљ иљ эсаљман ун хоят иты шушас. Хоят пеља аты аӈкармияс. Питљор эвие моштасљы, љув ищи таӈха вантсаљљы, хоты воељ хаљс. Па щи хољљап сура ёхтас. Турљ лап хащ ат катаљља, сэмьйиӈкаљн торастыман. Уртыељ вуты ёхатмаљн, љын пуӈљана иљ опсас. Унаӈкан ваныенан ищи ељ ёхи шушиљыман тата яӈхас. Љув ищи ант уятсаљљы, хоты няврэмљаља нётты. Ин љув хољыена ёнтты пиљ ант тайљат. Кашаŋ хоятљ там хотн саман воељ хоща карљасат. Хув машьяйн омассат. Ешавуљ сэмьйиŋкат нох сорсат, Юхур па ун хоят иты нох љоямтас, каман вер хољна мосаљ верты.

– Муя па муŋ воиев хаљас? – Питљор эвие хољна хољљапан ёхтамтыља. – Муя?

Етна пеља акайн, таљаŋ хатљ машьяйн уљман, апщеŋаљаљ пеља ястас:

– Ант мосас нёпиев хоят хота тутыя…

Унт вой утн уљты верљ уљ. Кашаŋ воен, кашаŋ хоятэн љув хот тайљ! Утн мосаŋ муŋ воев хув нупат ус. Хота сэма питс, щита љувељ мосас хайты. Амуя ёхи, хоят хота тусэм?

Title List

Igor Savitsky:
Artist, Collector, Museum Founder
by Marinika Babanazarova (2011)

Since the early 2000s, Igor Savitsky's life and accomplishments have earned increasing international recognition. He and the museum he founded in Nukus, the capital of Karakalpakstan in the far northwest of Uzbekistan. Marinika Babanazarova's memoir is based on her 1990 graduate dissertation at the Tashkent Theatre and Art Institute. It draws upon correspondence, official records, and other documents about the Savitsky family that have become available during the last few years, as well as the recollections of a wide range of people who knew Igor Savitsky personally.

Игорь Савитский: художник, собиратель, основатель музея

С начала 2000-х годов, жизнь и достижения Игоря Савицкого получили широкое признание во всем мире. Он и его музей, основанный в Нукусе, столице Каракалпакстана, стали предметом многочисленных статей в мировых газетах и журналах, таких как TheGuardian и NewYorkTimes, телевизионных программ в Австралии, Германии и Японии. Книга издана на русском, английском и французском языках.

Igor Savitski: Peintre, collectionneur, fondateur du Musée (French), (2012)

Le mémoire de Mme Babanazarova, basé sur sa thèse de 1990 à l'Institut de Théâtre et D'art de Tachkent, s'appuie sur la correspondance, les dossiers officiels et d'autres documents d'Igor Savitsky et de sa famille, qui sont devenus disponibles dernièrement, ainsi que sur les souvenirs de nombreuses personnes ayant connu Savistky personellement, ainsi que sur sa propre expérience de travail a ses cotés, en tant que successeur designé. son nom a titre posthume.

LANGUAGE: **ENG, RUS, FR** ISBN: **978-0955754999** RRP: **£10.00**
AVAILABLE ON **KINDLE**

Savitsky Collection Selected Masterpieces.
Poster set of 8 posters (2014)

Limited edition of prints from the world-renowned Museum of Igor Savitsky in Nukus, Uzbekistan. The set includs nine of the most famous works from the Savitsky collection wrapped in a colourful envelope. Selected Masterpieces of the Savitsky Collection.

[Cover] BullVasily Lysenko 1. Oriental Café Aleksei Isupov 2. Rendezvous Sergei Luppov 3. By the Sea. Marie-LouiseKliment Red'ko 4. Apocalypse Aleksei Rybnikov 5. Rain Irina Shtange 6. Purple Autumn Ural Tansykbayaev 7. To the Train Viktor Ufimtsev 8. Brigade to the fields Alexander Volkov This museum, also known as the Nukus Museum or the Savitsky

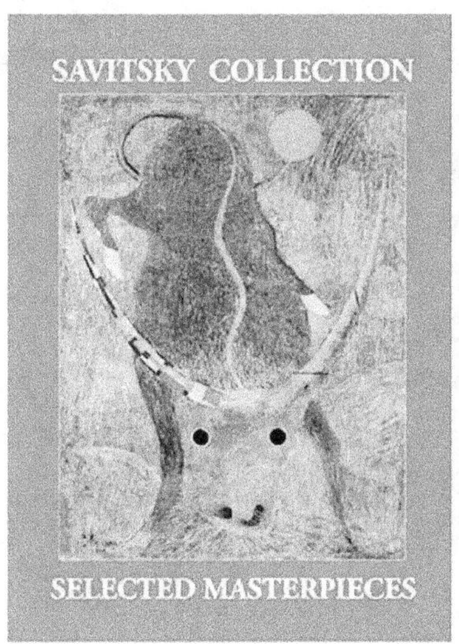

ISBN: **9780992787387**
RRP: **£25.00**

Friendly Steppes.
A Silk Road Journey
by Nick Rowan

This is the chronicle of an extraordinary adventure that led Nick Rowan to some of the world's most incredible and hidden places. Intertwined with the magic of 2,000 years of Silk Road history, he recounts his experiences coupled with a remarkable realisation of just what an impact this trade route has had on our society as we know it today. Containing colourful stories, beautiful photography and vivid characters, and wrapped in the local myths and legends told by the people Nick met and who live along the route, this is both a travelogue and an education of a part of the world that has remained hidden for hundreds of years.

HARD BACK ISBN: **978-0-9927873-4-9**
PAPERBACK ISBN: **978-0-9557549-4-4**
RRP: **£14.95**
AVAILABLE ON **KINDLE**

Birds of Uzbeksitan
by Nedosekov (2012)

FIRST
AND ONLY PHOTOALBUM
OF UZBEKISTAN BIRDS!

This book, which provides an introduction to the birdlife of Uzbekistan, is a welcome addition to the tools available to those working to conserve the natural heritage of the country. In addition to being the first photographic guide to the birds of Uzbekistan, the book is unique in only using photographs taken within the country. The compilers are to be congratulated on preparing an attractive and accessible work which hopefully will encourage more people to discover the rich birdlife of the country and want to protect it for future generations

HARD BACK
ISBN: **978-0-955754913**
RRP: **£25.00**

Pool of Stars
by Olesya Petrova,
Askar Urmanov,
English Edition (2007)

It is the first publication of a young writer Olesya Petrova, a talented and creative person. Fairy-tale characters dwell on this book's pages. Lovely illustrations make this book even more interesting to kids, thanks to a remarkable artist Askar Urmanov. We hope that our young readers will be very happy with such a gift. It's a book that everyone will appreciate. For the young, innocent ones - it's a good source of lessons they'll need in life. For the not-so-young but young at heart, it's a great book to remind us that life is so much more than work.

ISBN: **978-0955754906** **ENGLISH** AVAILABLE ON **KINDLE**

«Звёздная лужица»

Первая книга для детей, изданная британским издательством Hertfordshire Press. Это также первая публикация молодой талантливой писательницы Олеси Петровой. Сказочные персонажи живут на страницах этой книги. Прекрасные иллюстрации делают книгу еще более интересной и красочной для детей, благодаря замечательному художнику Аскару Урманову. Вместе Аскар и Олеся составляют удивительный творческий тандем, который привнес жизнь в эту маленькую книгу

ISBN: **978-0955754906** **RUSSIAN**
RRP: **£4.95**

Buyuk Temurhon (Tamerlane)
by C. Marlowe,
Uzbek Edition (2010)

Hertfordshire based publisher Silk Road Media, run by Marat Akhmedjanov, and the BBC Uzbek Service have published one of Christopher Marlowe's famous plays, Tamburlaine the Great, translated into the Uzbek language. It is the first of Christopher Marlowe's plays to be translated into Uzbek, which is Tamburlaine's native language. Translated by Hamid Ismailov, the current BBC World Service Writer-in-Residence, this new publication seeks to introduce English classics to Uzbek readers worldwide.

PAPERBACK
ISBN: **9780955754982**
RRP: **£10.00**
AVAILABLE ON **KINDLE**

Under Wolf's Nest
by KairatZakiryanov
English –Kazakh edition

Were the origins of Islam, Christianity and the legend of King Arthur all influenced by steppe nomads from Kazakhstan? Ranging through thousands of years of history, and drawing on sources from Herodotus through to contemporary Kazakh and Russian research, the crucial role in the creation of modern civilisation played by the Turkic people is revealed in this detailed yet highly accessible work. Professor Kairat Zakiryanov, President of the Kazakh Academy of Sport and Tourism, explains how generations of steppe nomads, including Genghis Khan, have helped shape the language, culture and populations of Asia, Europe, the Middle East and America through migrations taking place over millennia.

HARD BACK
ISBN: **9780957480728**
RRP: **£17.50**
AVAILABLE ON **KINDLE**

When Edelweiss flowers flourish
by Begenas Saratov
English edition (2012)

A spectacular insight into life in the Soviet Union in the late 1960's made all the more intriguing by its setting within the Sovet Republic of Kyrgyzstan. The story explores Soviet life, traditional Kyrgyz life and life on planet Earth through a Science Fiction story based around an alien nations plundering of the planet for life giving herbs. The author reveals far sighted thoughts and concerns for conservation, management of natural resources and dialogue to achieve peace yet at the same time shows extraordinary foresight with ideas for future technologies and the progress of science. The whole style of the writing gives a fascinating insight into the many facets of life in a highly civilised yet rarely known part of the world.

ISBN: **978-0955754951** **PAPERBACK** AVAILABLE ON **KINDLE**

Mamyry gyldogon maalda

Это фантастический рассказ, повествующий о советской жизни, жизни кыргызского народа и о жизни на планете в целом. Автор рассказывает об инопланетных народах, которые пришли на нашу планету, чтобы разграбить ее. Автор раскрывает дальновидность мысли о сохранение и рациональном использовании природных ресурсов, а также диалога для достижения мира и в то же время показывает необычайную дальновидность с идеями для будущих технологий и прогресса науки. Книга также издана на **кыргызском языке**.

ISBN: **97809555754951**
RRP: **£12.95**

Tales from Bush House
(BBC Wolrd Service)
by Hamid Ismailov
(2012)

Tales From Bush House is a collection of short narratives about working lives, mostly real and comic, sometimes poignant or apocryphal, gifted to the editors by former and current BBC World Service employees. They are tales from inside Bush House - the home of the World Service since 1941 - escaping through its marble-clad walls at a time when its staff begin their departure to new premises in Portland Place. In July 2012, the grand doors of this imposing building will close on a vibrant chapter in the history of Britain's most cosmopolitan organisation. So this is a timely book.

PAPERBACK
ISBN: **9780955754975**
RRP: **£12.95**
AVAILABLE ON **KINDLE**

Chants of Dark Fire
(Песни темного огня)
by Zhulduz Baizakova
Russian edition (2012)

This contemporary work of poetry contains the deep and inspirational rhythms of the ancient Steppe. It combines the nomad, modern, postmodern influences in Kazakhstani culture in the early 21st century, and reveals the hidden depths of contrasts, darkness, and longing for light that breathes both ice and fire to inspire a rich form of poetry worthy of reading and contemplating. It is also distinguished by the uniqueness of its style and substance. Simply sublime, it has to be read and felt for real.

ISBN: **978-0957480711**
RRP: **£10.00**

Kamila
by R. Karimov
Kyrgyz – Uzbek Edition (2013)

«Камила» - это история о сироте, растущей на юге Кыргызстана. Наряду с личной трагедией Камилы и ее родителей, Рахим Каримов описывает очень реалистично и подробно местный образ жизни. Роман выиграл конкурс "Искусство книги-2005" в Бишкеке и был признан национальным бестселлером Книжной палаты Кыргызской Республики.

PAPERBACK
ISBN: **978-0957480773**
RRP: **£10.00**

Gods of the Middle World
by Galina Dolgaya (2013)

The Gods of the Middle World tells the story of Sima, a student of archaeology for whom the old lore and ways of the Central Asian steppe peoples are as vivid as the present. When she joints a group of archaeologists in southern Kazakhstan, asking all the time whether it is really possible to 'commune with the spirits', she soon discovers the answer first hand, setting in motion events in the spirit world that have been frozen for centuries. Meanwhile three millennia earlier, on the same spot, a young woman and her companion struggle to survive and amend wrongs that have caused the neighbouring tribe to take revenge. The two narratives mirror one another, and Sima's destiny is to resolve the ancient wrongs in her own lifetime and so restore the proper balance of the forces of good and evil

PAPERBACK
ISBN: **978-0957480797**
RRP: **£14.95**
AVAILABLE ON **KINDLE**

Jazz Book, poetry
by Alma Sharipova , Russian Edition

Сборник стихов Алмы Шариповой JazzCafé, в котором предлагаются стихотворения, написанные в разное время и посвященые различным событиям из жизни автора.

Стихотворения Алмы содержательные и эмоциональные одновременно, отражают философию ее отношения к происходящему. Почти каждое стихотворение представляет собой законченный рассказ в миниатюре. Сюжет разворачивается последовательно и завершается небольшим резюме в последних строках. Стихотворения раскрываются, как готовые «формулы» жизни. Читатель невольно задумывается над ними и может найти как что-то знакомое, так и новое для себя.

ISBN: **978-0-957480797**
RRP: **£10.00**

13 steps of Erika Klaus
by Kazat Akmatov (2013)

The story involves the harrowing experiences of a young and very naïve Norwegian woman who has come to Kyrgyzstan to teach English to schoolchildren in a remote mountain outpost. Governed by the megalomaniac Colonel Bronza, the community barely survives under a cruel and unjust neo-fascist regime. Immersed in the local culture, Erika is initially both enchanted and apprehensive but soon becomes disillusioned as day after day, she is forbidden to teach. Alongside Erika's story, are the personal tragedies experienced by former soldier Sovietbek , Stalbek, the local policeman, the Principal of the school and a young man who has married a Kyrgyz refugee from Afghanistan . Each tries in vain, to challenge and change the corrupt political situation in which they are forced to live.

PAPERBACK
ISBN: **978-0957480766**
RRP: **£12.95**
AVAILABLE ON **KINDLE**

The Modernization of Foreign Language Education: The Linguocultural - Communicative Approach
by SalimaKunanbayeva (2013)

Professor S. S. Kunanbayeva - Rector of Ablai Khan Kazakh University of International Relations and World Languages This textbook is the first of its kind in Kazakhstan to be devoted to the theory and practice of foreign language education. It has been written primarily for future teachers of foreign languages and in a wider sense for all those who to be interested in the question (in the problems?) of the study and use of foreign languages. This book outlines an integrated theory of modern foreign language learning (FLL) which has been drawn up and approved under the auspices of the school of science and methodology of Kazakhstan's Ablai Khan University of International Relations and World Languages.

PAPERBACK
ISBN: **978-0957480780**
RRP: **£19.95**
AVAILABLE ON **KINDLE**

Shahidka/ Munabia
by KazatAkmatov (2013)

Munabiya and Shahidka by Kazat Akmatov National Writer of Kyrgyzstan Recently translated into English Akmatov's two love stories are set in rural Kyrgyzstan, where the natural environment, local culture, traditions and political climate all play an integral part in the dramas which unfold. Munabiya is a tale of a family's frustration, fury, sadness and eventual acceptance of a long term love affair between the widowed father and his mistress. In contrast, Shahidka is a multi-stranded story which focuses on the ties which bind a series of individuals to the tragic and ill-fated union between a local Russian girl and her Chechen lover, within a multi-cultural community where violence, corruption and propaganda are part of everyday life.

PAPERBACK
ISBN: **978-0957480759**
RRP: **£12.95**
AVAILABLE ON **KINDLE**

Howl *novel*
by Kazat Akmatov (2014)
English –Russian

The “Howl” by Kazat Akmatov is a beautifully crafted novel centred on life in rural Kyrgyzstan. Characteristic of the country’s national writer, the simple plot is imbued with descriptions of the spectacular landscape, wildlife and local customs. The theme however, is universal and the contradictory emotions experienced by Kalen the shepherd must surely ring true to young men, and their parents, the world over. Here is a haunting and sensitively written story of a bitter -sweet rite of passage from boyhood to manhood.

PAPERBACK
ISBN: **978-0993044410**
RRP: **£12.50**
AVAILABLE ON **KINDLE**

The Turkic Saga of Genghis Khan and the KZ Factor
by Dr.Kairat Zakiryanov (2014)

An in-depth study of Genghis Khan from a Kazakh perspective, The Turkic Saga of Genghis Khan presupposes that the great Mongol leader and his tribal setting had more in common with the ancestors of the Kazakhs than with the people who today identify as Mongols. This idea is growing in currency in both western and eastern scholarship and is challenging both old Western assumptions and the long-obsolete Soviet perspective. This is an academic work that draws on many Central Asian and Russian sources and often has a Eurasianist bias - while also paying attention to new accounts by Western authors such as Jack Weatherford and John Man. It bears the mark of an independent, unorthodox and passionate scholar.

HARD BACK
ISBN: **978-0992787370**
RRP: **£17.50**
AVAILABLE ON **KINDLE**

Alphabet Game
by Paul Wilson (2014)

Travelling around the world may appear as easy as ABC, but looks can be deceptive: there is no 'X' for a start. Not since Xidakistan was struck from the map. Yet post 9/11, with the War on Terror going global, could 'The Valley' be about to regain its place on the political stage? Xidakistan's fate is inextricably linked with that of Graham Ruff, founder of Ruff Guides. Setting sail where Around the World in Eighty Days and Lost Horizon weighed anchor, our not-quite-a-hero suffers all in pursuit of his golden triangle: The Game, The Guidebook, The Girl. With the future of printed Guidebooks increasingly in question, As Evelyn Waugh's Scoop did for Foreign Correspondents the world over, so this novel lifts the lid on Travel Writers for good.

PAPERBACK
ISBN: **978-0-992787325**
RRP: **£14.95**
AVAILABLE ON **KINDLE**

Life over pain and desperation
by Marziya Zakiryanova (2014)

This book was written by someone on the fringe of death. Her life had been split in two: before and after the first day of August 1991 when she, a mother of two small children and full of hopes and plans for the future, became disabled in a single twist of fate. Narrating her tale of self-conquest, the author speaks about how she managed to hold her family together, win the respect and recognition of people around her and above all, protect the fragile concept of 'love' from fortune's cruel turns. By the time the book was submitted to print, Marziya Zakiryanova had passed away. She died after making the last correction to her script. We bid farewell to this remarkable and powerfully creative woman.

HARD BACK
ISBN: **978-0-99278733-2**
RRP: **£14.95**
AVAILABLE ON **KINDLE**

100 experiences of Kazakhstan
by Vitaly Shuptar, Nick Rowan and Dagmar Schreiber (2014)

The original land of the nomads, landlocked Kazakhstan and its expansive steppes present an intriguing border between Europe and Asia. Dispel the notion of oil barons and Borat and be prepared for a warm welcome into a land full of contrasts. A visit to this newly independent country will transport you to a bygone era to discover a country full of legends and wonders. Whether searching for the descendants of Genghis Khan - who left his mark on this land seven hundred years ago - or looking to discover the futuristic architecture of its capital Astana, visitors cannot fail but be impressed by what they experience. For those seeking adventure, the formidable Altai and Tien Shan mountains provide challenges for novices and experts alike

ISBN: **978-0-992787356**
RRP: **£19.95**

Dance of Devils , Jinlar Bazmi
by AbdulhamidIsmoil
and Hamid Ismailov
(Uzbek language),
E-book (2012)

'Dance of Devils' is a novel about the life of a great Uzbek writer Abdulla Qadyri (incidentally, 'Dance of Devils' is the name of one of his earliest short stories). In 1937, Qadyri was going to write a novel, which he said was to make his readers to stop reading his iconic novels "Days Bygone" and "Scorpion from the altar," so beautiful it would have been. The novel would've told about a certain maid, who became a wife of three Khans - a kind of Uzbek Helen of Troy. He told everyone: "I will sit down this winter and finish this novel - I have done my preparatory work, it remains only to write. Then people will stop reading my previous books". He began writing this novel, but on the December 31, 1937 he was arrested.

AVAILABLE ON **KINDLE**
ASIN: B009ZBPV2M

Vanished Khans and Empty Steppes by Robert Wight (2014)

The book opens with an outline ofthehistoryofAlmaty,fromitsnineteenth-century origins as a remote outpost of the Russian empire, up to its present status as the thriving second city of modern-day Kazakhstan. The story then goes back to the Neolithic and early Bronze Ages, and the sensational discovery of the famous Golden Man of the Scythian empire. The transition has been difficult and tumultuous for millions of people, but Vanished Khans and Empty Steppes illustrates how Kazakhstan has emerged as one of the world's most successful post-communist countries.

HARD BACK
ISBN: **978-0-9930444-0-3**
RRP: **£24.95**

PAPERBACK
ISBSN: **978-1-910886-05-2**
RRP: **£14.50**
AVAILABLE ON **KINDLE**

Man of the Mountains
by Abudlla Isa (2014)
(OCABF 2013 Winner)

Man of the Mountains" is a book about a young Muslim Chechen boy, Zaur who becomes a central figure representing the fight of local indigenous people against both the Russians invading the country and Islamic radicals trying to take a leverage of the situation, using it to push their narrow political agenda on the eve of collapse of the USSR. After 9/11 and the invasion of Iraq and Afghanistan by coalition forces, the subject of the Islamic jihadi movement has become an important subject for the Western readers. But few know about the resistance movement from the local intellectuals and moderates against radical Islamists taking strong hold in the area.

PAPERBACK
ISBN: **978-0-9930444-5-8**
RRP: **£14.95**
AVAILABLE ON **KINDLE**

Silk, Spice, Veils and Vodka
by Felicity Timcke (2014)

Felicity Timcke's missive publication, "Silk, Spices, Veils and Vodka" brings both a refreshing and new approach to life on the expat trail. South African by origin, Timcke has lived in some very exotic places, mostly along the more challenging countries of the Silk Road. Although the book's content, which is entirely composed of letters to the author's friends and family, is directed primarily at this group, it provides "20 years of musings" that will enthral and delight those who have either experienced a similar expatriate existence or who are nervously about to depart for one.

PAPERBACK
ISBN: **978-0992787318**
RRP: **£12.50**
AVAILABLE ON **KINDLE**

Finding the Holy Path
by Shahsanem Murray (2014)

"Murray's first book provides an enticing and novel link between her adopted home town of Edinburgh and her origins form Central Asia. Beginning with an investigation into a mysterious lamp that turns up in an antiques shop in Edinburgh, and is bought on impulse, we are quickly brought to the fertile Ferghana valley in Uzbekistan to witness the birth of Kara-Choro, and the start of an enthralling story that links past and present. Told through a vivid and passionate dialogue, this is a tale of parallel discovery and intrigue. The beautifully translated text, interspersed by regional poetry, cannot fail to impress any reader, especially those new to the region who will be affectionately drawn into its heart in this page-turning cultural thriller."

В поисках святого перевала – удивительный приключенческий роман, основанный на исторических источниках. Произведение Мюррей – это временной мостик между эпохами, который помогает нам переместиться в прошлое и уносит нас далеко в 16 век. Закрученный сюжет предоставляет нам уникальную возможность, познакомиться с историейи культурой Центральной Азии. «Первая книга Мюррей предлагает заманчивый роман, связывающий между её приемным городом Эдинбургом и Центральной Азией, откуда настоящее происхождение автора.

RUS ISBN: **978-0-9930444-8-9**
ENGL ISBN: **978-0992787394**
PAPERBACK
RRP: **£12.50**

Azerbaijan:
Bridge between East and West
by Yury Sigov, 2015

Azerbaijan: Bridge between East and West, Yury Sigov narrates a comprehensive and compelling story about Azerbaijan. He balances the country's rich cultural heritage, wonderful people and vibrant environment with its modern political and economic strategies. Readers will get the chance to thoroughly explore Azerbaijan from many different perspectives and discover a plethora of innovations and idea, including the recipe for Azerbaijan's success as a nation and its strategies for the future. The book also explores the history of relationships between United Kingdom and Azerbaijan.

HARD BACK
ISBN: **978-0-9930444-9-6**
RRP: **£24.50**
AVAILABLE ON **KINDLE**

Kashmir Song
by Sharaf Rashidov
(translation by Alexey Ulko, OCABF 2014 Winner). 2015

This beautiful illustrated novella offers a sensitive reworking of an ancient and enchanting folk story which although rooted in Kashmir is, by nature of its theme, universal in its appeal.

Alternative interpretations of this tale are explored by Alexey Ulko in his introduction, with references to both politics and contemporary literature, and the author's epilogue further reiterates its philosophical dimension.

The Kashmir Song is a timeless tale, which true to the tradition of classical folklore, can be enjoyed on a number of levels by readers of all ages.

COMING SOON!!!
ISBN: 978-0-9930444-2-7
RRP: £29.50

Land of forty tribes
by Farideh Heyat, 2015

Sima Omid, a British-Iranian anthropologist in search of her Turkic roots, takes on a university teaching post in Kyrgyzstan. It is the year following 9/11, when the US is asserting its influence in the region. Disillusioned with her long-standing relationship, Sima is looking for a new man in her life. But the foreign men she meets are mostly involved in relationships with local women half their age, and the Central Asian men she finds highly male chauvinist and aggressive towards women.

PAPERBACK
ISBN: **978-0-9930444-4-1**
RRP: **£14.95**

Terror: events, facts, evidence.
by Eldar Samadov, 2015

This book is based on research carried out since 1988 on territorial claims of Armenia against Azerbaijan, which led to the escalation of the conflict over Nagorno-Karabakh. This escalation included acts of terror by Armanian terrorist and other armed gangs not only in areas where intensive armed confrontations took place but also away from the fighting zones. This book, not for the first time, reflects upon the results of numerous acts of premeditated murder, robbery, armed attack and other crimes through collected material related to criminal cases which have been opened at various stages following such crimes. The book is meant for political scientists, historians, lawyers, diplomats and a broader audience.

PAPERBACK
ISBN: **978-1-910886-00-7**
RRP: **£9.99**
AVAILABLE ON **KINDLE**

THE PLIGHT OF A POSTMODERN HUNTER
Chlngiz Aitmatov
Mukhtar Shakhanov
(2015)

"Delusion of civilization" by M. Shakhanov is an epochal poem, rich in prudence and nobility – as is his foremother steppe. It is the voice of the Earth, which raised itself in defense of the human soul. This is a new genre of spiritual ecology. As such, this book is written from the heart of a former tractor driver, who knows all the "scars and wrinkles" of the soil - its thirst for human intimacy. This book is also authored from the perspective of an outstanding intellectual whose love for national traditions has grown as universal as our common great motherland.

I dare say, this book is a spiritual instrument of patriotism for all humankind. Hence, there is something gentle, kind, and sad, about the old swan-song of Mukhtar's brave ancestors. Those who for six months fought to the death to protect Grand Otrar - famous worldwide for its philosophers and rich library, from the hordes of Genghis Khan.

LANGUAGES ENG
HARDBACK
ISBN: **978-1-910886-11-3**
RRP: **£24.95**
AVAILABLE ON **KINDLE**

The Wormwood Wind
Raushan
Burkitbayeva- Nukenova
(2015)

A single unstated assertion runs throughout The Wormwood Wind, arguing, amid its lyrical nooks and crannies, we are only fully human when our imaginations are free. Possibly this is the primary glittering insight behind Nukenova's collaboration with hidden Restorative Powers above her pen. No one would doubt, for example, when she hints that the moment schoolchildren read about their surrounding environment they are acting in a healthy and developmental manner. Likewise, when she implies any adult who has the courage to think "outside the box" quickly gains a reputation for adaptability in their private affairs – hardly anyone would doubt her. General affirmations demonstrating this sublime and liberating contribution to Global Text will prove dangerous to unwary readers, while its intoxicating rhythms and rhymes will lead a grateful few to elative revolutions inside their own souls. Thus, I unreservedly recommend this ingenious work to Western readers.

HARD BACK
ISBN: **978-1-910886-12-0**
RRP: **£14.95**
AVAILABLE ON **KINDLE**

"Cranes in Spring"
by Tolibshohi Davlat
(2015)

This novel highlights a complex issue that millions of Tajiks face when becoming working migrants in Russia due to lack of opportunities at home. Fresh out of school, Saidakbar decides to go to Russia as he hopes to earn money to pay for his university tuition. His parents reluctantly let him go providing he is accompanied by his uncle, Mustakim, an experienced migrant. And so begins this tale of adventure and heartache that reflects the reality of life faced by many Central Asian migrants. Mistreatment, harassment and backstabbing join the Tajik migrants as they try to pull through in a foreign country. Davlat vividly narrates the brutality of the law enforcement officers but also draws attention to kindness and help of several ordinary people in Russia. How will Mustakim and Saidakbar's journey end? Intrigued by the story starting from the first page, one cannot put the book down until it's finished.

LANGUAGES ENG / RUS
HARDBACK
ISBN: **978-1-910886-06-9**
RRP: **£14.50**

"Tvorcheskoe Sodrujestvo"
first edition
(2015)

«Творческое содружество» - это объемное издание в твердом переплете, состоящее из 500 страниц, которое включает в себя отчетный дайджест по Третьему Международному Литературному Фестивалю и Книжному Форуму «Open Eurasia and Central Asia book forum and literature festival - 2014».

В издании опубликованы фрагменты из произведений гостей фестиваля, финалистов и победителей конкурса, литературная критика, информация о мероприятиях и новинках издательства Hertfordshire Press.

LANGUAGES RUS
PAPERBACK
ISBN: **978-1910886014**
RRP: **£17.50**
HARDBACK
ISBN: **978-1910886083**
RRP: **£20**

The novel "Arhat"
by Kazat Akmatov
(2015)

The novel "Arhat" by the Kyrgyz writer Kazat Akmatov was presented in Moscow at the International Festival "Bibliobraz - 2007" in the Kyrgyz, Russian and Bulgarian languages. Then, the novel was introduced to public in New Delhi at the World Buddhist Congress as well as in a city Drahsalam where the Tibetan Dalai Lama XIV lives. The novel has been translated into English and other languages. "Arhat" caused a wide resonance at home and was awarded by a number of national and international awards as well recognized the best novel and the "National bestseller of 2007". In the novel, it is a deal of the destiny of the Kyrgyz boy - the reincarnation of the great Tibetan Lama and poet who lived a thousand years ago…

LANGUAGES ENG
PAPERBACK
ISBN: **978-1910886106**
RRP: **£17.50**

"The Great Melody"
by Tabyldy Aktan
(2015)

"The Great Melody" is a musical drama by Tabyldy Aktan. This book is dedicated to the memory and the 150th anniversary of the great Kyrgyz bard Toktogul Satylganov. Toktogul Satulganov the Kyrgyz bard, philosopher, democrat, composer and skilled player of his country"s national instrument, the komuz, was born in 1864 in SazJuide, a village in the KetmenTobo area. In 2014 the book was translated into English by Zina Karaeva, the Director of the Institute of Foreign Languages at the International University of Kyrgyzstan.

LANGUAGES ENG
ISBN: **978-1-910886-02-1**
RRP: **£3.24**
AVAILABLE ON **KINDLE**

The Taste of Central asia Cook book

by Danny Gordon

(2015)

This is a culinary guide to Central Asia, divided by city and decorated with colourful images. This book is a perfect gift for those who want to discover the Central Asian region and be inspired to make new travels and gain new experiences.

LANGUAGES ENG

PAPERBACK

ISBN: **978-1-910886-09-0**

RRP: **£19.95**

COMING SOON

"Guardian of treasures"
by Maksim.Karsakov
(2015)

Maxim Korsakov's novella The Hollywood Conundrum or Guardian of Treasure simply refuses to acknowledge these dis-empowering parameters in anything other than the most vigorous terms. Frivolously playing, as it does, with genre expectations, and delighting in a highly crafted sensationalism. Twin techniques augmented throughout this ingenious work by Korsakov's use of texture, colour, taste, temperature, size and fleshliness. Divided into two parts, his initial tale explores the false nirvana masking marriages of convenience. A so-called "biographical" account reading like a masterclass in the muted horrors of selfimposed delusion. Immediately following, intrigued readers will discover a "script", which would easily put most James Bond screenplays to shame..

LANGUAGES ENG / RUSS
PAPERBACK
ISBN: **978-1-910886-14-4**
RRP: **£24.95**

Goethe and Abai
by Herold Berger
(2015)

Present publication of Herold Berger's personal and scholarly essay on these two giants of world literature. Berger's unique stance is to follow the dictates of his imagination, inspired by a close life-long study of Goethe and Abai, and, alongside many detailed scholarly investigations, e.g. his comparative study of Goethe and Abai's innovations in poetic metre, form and consonance, or of the sources and background of Goethe's Eastern inspired masterpiece West-East Divan, Berger muses openly about the personal impact that Goethe and Abai have had on him.

LANGUAGES ENG
HARDBACK
ISBN: **978-1-910886-16-8**
RRP: **£17.50**

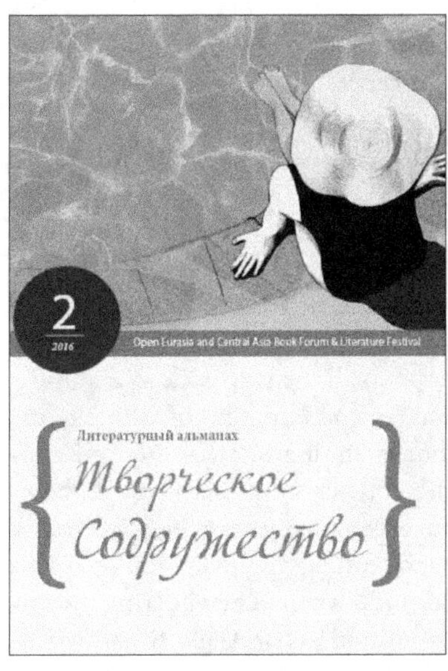

“Tvorcheskoe sodrujestvo-2”
second edition
(2016)

This book is a unified voice of our generation - young and talented authors of different ethnic and cultural backgrounds. By opening this book, you discover a new artistic word, the word of writers which will pass through generations. “Creative Cooperation” reflects the literary contest «Open Eurasia and Central Asia Book Forum & Literature Festival» and seeks to enlighten, promote, and recognize the region’s talents and their invaluable work.

LANGUAGES RUSS
PAPERBACK
ISBN: **978-1-910886-21-2**
RRP: **£20**

The Grammar of Witchcraft
David Parry
(2016)

In this collection of Mini-Sagas and poems, Parry narrates the final journey taken by his alter ego Caliban from the surreal delights of a lesbian wedding in Liverpool, all the way back to a non-existent city of London. In himself, the author is aiming to resolve lyrical contradictions existing between different levels of consciousness: betwixt reality and the dreaming state. And as such, unnervingly illogical scenarios emerge out of a stream of consciousness wherein bewildering theatrical landscapes actively compete with notions of Anglo-Saxon witchcraft, Radical Traditionalism, and a lack of British authenticity. Each analysis pointing towards those Jungian Spirits haunting an endlessly benevolent Archetypal world.

LANGUAGES ENG
PAPERBACK
ISBN: **978-1-910886-25-0**
RRP: **£9.95**

The City Where Dreams Come True
Gulsifat Shahidi
(2016)

Viewed from the perspective of three generations, Shahidi presents a rare and poignant insight into the impact which Tajikistan'sterrible civil war had on its people and its culture during the early '90s. Informed partly by her own experiences as a journalist, these beautifully interwoven stories are imbued with both her affection for her native land and her hopes for its future. The narrators – Horosho, his granddaughter Nekbaht ,her husband Ali and his cousin Shernazar – each endure harrowing episodes of loss, injustice and violence but against all odds, remain driven by a will to survive, and restore peace, prosperity and new opportunities for themselves and fellow citizens.

LANGUAGES ENG / RUS
PAPERBACK
ISBN: **978-1-910886-20-5**
RRP: **£12.50**

Crane
Abu-Sufyan
(2016)

In this remarkable collection of prose poems, author Abu Sufyan takes readers through a series of fairy tale scenarios, wherein are hidden a number of sour existential truths. Indeed, from the bewilderment felt by anthropomorphised cranes, to the self-sacrifice of mares galloping towards their (potential) salvation, all the way to the bittersweet biographies experienced by a girl and her frustrated mother, this book weaves darkly enchanted frame stories into highly illustrative fables. Structured, as they are, in the style of unfolding dialogues, Sufyan's haunting literary technique serves to unveil a story within a storyline. An almost Postmodern strategy, whereby an introductory, or main narrative, is presented (at least in part), for the sole purpose of sharing uncomfortable anecdotes. As such, critics have observed that emphasized secondary yarns allow readers to find themselves - so to speak - stepping from one theme into another - while simultaneously being carried into ever-smaller plots. Certainly, as adventures take place between named and memorable characters, each exchange is saturated with wit, practical jokes, and life lessons contributing to an overall Central Asian literary mosaic. All in all, this tiny volume is both a delight and a warning to its admirers.

LANGUAGES ENG
PAPERBACK
ISBN: **978-1-910886-23-6**
RRP: **£12.50**

My Homeland, Oh My Crimea
by Lenifer Mambetova
(2015)

Mambetova's delightful poems, exploring the hopes and fates of Crimean Tartars, are a timely and evocative reminder of how deep a people's roots can be, but also how adaptable and embracing foreigners can be of their adopted country, its people and its traditions.

LANGUAGES ENG / RUS
HARDBACK
ISBN: **978-1-910886-04-5**

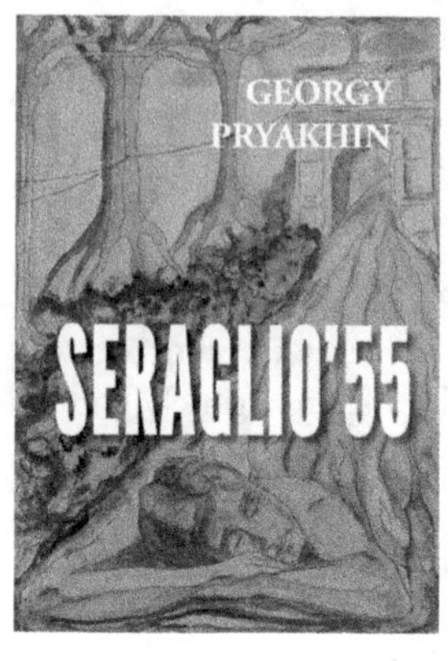

SERAGLIO'55
Georgy Pryakhin
(2016)

This is a wonderful publication, full of Georgy Pryakhin's personal recollectionsofalifetimespentnotonly as one of the most revered Russian writers but as a political supremo in the inner circle of the Gorbachev government during the last years of the USSR. It will enchant readers with a thirst to learn more of the inner workings of those who lived through the USSR, Glasnost and Perestroika. Pryakhin's vivid recollections of real events, idealistic dreams and his way of seeing life, tell stories that go much deeper than the words printed on the page. Born in 1947 to mixed Uzbek and Russian parents exiled and killed by Stalin's brutal regime, he grew up in a Stalin orphanage to see the very worst of life in Russia and its internal conflicts, which moulded his desire to tell the world through his writing about what he had seen, heard and felt, which he later translated into how he could help others through working in politics to change the life of Russians for the better, forever. Pryakhin's stories, told in the present tense, give the reader every feeling of what it was like to be there at this most important of times in Russia's recent history and are a rare insight into the workings and machinations of life at the top during colossal societal changes. I am delighted to be able to introduce and recommend this worthy publication

LANGUAGES ENG
PAPERBACK
ISBN: 978-1-910886-28-1
RRP: £14.50

REPENTANCE
Yermek Amanshaev
(2016)

'Repentance' is a poignant collection of three short stories- 'Song of Laments', 'Futility' and 'Repentance' – which explore the psychological complexity of relationships between fathers and sons.

The issues addressed are ageless and universal. Set across the centuries, from biblical times to the present, often merging mythology with illusion and reality, the stories focus on challenges faced by fathers and sons as each struggles to assert his own identity and individual place in the world

Amanshayev 's prose is wonderfully visual, providing theatrical settings which are further enhanced by a rhythmic use of words to conjure sound; from the melodic dombra to the cries of the animals and winds of the Steppe,and the beat of a bouncing ball. His characters are portrayed with equal sensitivity, from the young warrior, the new father and suicidal son, each caught up in a 'boundless twilight of loneliness', to the homeless addicts, spurned women and Lothario father; each one inviting empathy from the reader.

LANGUAGES ENG
PAPERBACK
ISBN: 978-1-910886-33-5
RRP: £14.95

COLD SHADOWS
Shahsanem Murray
(2016)

The story, set at the end of the 1980's, revolves around a group of disparate individuals living seemingly unconnected lives in various countries.

But then a strange incident on the Moscow to Frunze train leads to the gradual exposure of complex web in which their lives, loves and profession's have long been entangled.

Bound together by an intriguing series of incidents, each struggles to survive the hardships and challenges that life throws at them, from radical changes in the political climate to the murky antics of spies and double agents. But behind everything lies love…

LANGUAGES ENG
PAPERBACK
ISBN: 978-1-910886-27-4
RRP: **£12.50**

HEIRS TO THE GREAT SINNER SHEIKH SAN'ON
Erkin A'zam
(2016)

Erkin A'zam's book in English comprises two novellas, The Din and A Tender-hearted Dwarf, and two short stories, The Writer's Garden and A dog bit the Incomer's Daughter, which previously have been published by the Uzbek representative office of UNESCO under the title Farewell to Fairy Tales. The newly-translated novella Gooli-Gooli is published for the first time.

Heirs to the Great Sinner Sheikh San'on opens a window onto what life was like in Uzbekistan in the recent past, and shows the reader what it means to be an Uzbek man or woman today. As one author and critic puts it:
"Nothing is eternal in this rapidly-changing, globalized world: time hurtles on, political systems rise and fall, the ever-hungry din roars on, inside and out, and all this takes its toll on each and every one of us. Only human nature and the soul remain unshakeable – this is the main message of."

LANGUAGES ENG
ISBN:978-1-910886-32-8
PAPER BACK
PRICE: £14.95

DOES IT YURT?
Stephen M. Bland
(2016)

Conjuring images of nomadic horsemen, spectacular monuments, breathtaking scenery and crippling poverty, Central Asia remains an enigma. Home to the descendants of Jenghiz Khan's Great Horde, in the nineteenth century the once powerful Silk Road states became a pawn in the 'Great Game' of expansion and espionage between Britain and Russia, disappearing behind what would become known as the 'Iron Curtain'. With the collapse of the USSR, the nations of Kazakhstan, Kyrgyzstan, Tajikistan, Turkmenistan and Uzbekistan were born. Since independence, Central Asia has seen one civil war, two revolutions and seven dictators.

An insightful mix of travel, history and reportage, in Does it Yurt? journalist Stephen M. Bland takes the reader on a voyage of discovery. Travelling to a desert sea, a collapsed Russian gas rig daubed the 'Gate to Hell' and along the 'Heroin highway' atop the roof of the world, the author sets out to explore these lands, unearthing the stories of the people and places behind this fascinating region.

LANGUAGES ENG
PAPER BACK
RRP:14.95
ISBN: 978-1-910886-29-8

SHADOWS OF THE RAIN
Raushan
Burkitbayeva - Nukenova
(2016)

In this bold and insightful second collection of Neo-Expressionist literatures, Raushan Burkit Bayeva-Nukenova invites her readers to revel in the cogitations of a Kazakh Radical Traditionalist. A literary position provoking the exploration of Eurasian motives, Central Asian reactions to London, nomadic love, and the contours of ethnic memory. Each one of which is lyrically scrutinized - along with the dissonant place of women in our postmodern world. Indeed, unlike her highly successful and probing first volume The Wormwood Wind, the author of this present book seeks to extend her poetic analysis of current affairs, before taking her first tentative footsteps into prose. This may be why pundits are already saying that several diverse strains of autobiographical text stream throughout this fresh and innovative work. All explaining, of course, the obvious value of such a tome as a unique contribution to those literary discernments mapping contemporary femininities exact boundaries. Unarguably, therefore, Raushan Burkit Bayeva-Nukenova's examination of nationality, colour, religion, and cultural backgrounds, will both challenge the assumptions of Western readers, while opening the doors of perception into a uniquely Central Asian perspective.

LANGUAGES ENG
HARD BACK
RRP:19.95
ISBN: 978-1-910886-31-1

The literary work "Blue River" by Khanty writer Zinaida Longortova was recognized as the best work in the literary competition as a part of the Fourth International Literary Festival
Open Eurasia Book Forum & Literature Festival - 2015

published by

www.ingramcontent.com/pod-product-compliance
Lightning Source LLC
Chambersburg PA
CBHW060547310726
48982CB00008B/1044/J

* 9 7 8 1 9 1 0 8 8 6 3 4 2 *